The Space of Love

Anastasia herself has stated that this book consists of words and phrases in combinations *which have a beneficial effect on the reader.* This has been attested by the letters received to date from tens of thousands of readers all over the world.

If you wish to gain as full an appreciation as possible of the ideas, thoughts and images set forth here, as well as experience the benefits that come with this appreciation, we recommend you find a quiet place for your reading where there is the least possible interference from artificial noises (motor traffic, radio, TV, household appliances etc.). *Natural sounds,* on the other hand — the singing of birds, for example, or the patter of rain, or the rustle of leaves on nearby trees — may be a welcome accompaniment to the reading process.

THE RINGING CEDARS SERIES • BOOK THREE

3

The Space of Love

Vladimir Megré

Translated from the Russian by John Woodsworth
Edited by Dr Leonid Sharashkin

RINGING
CEDARS
PRESS

KAHULUI • HAWAII • USA

Mixed Sources
Product group from well-managed
forests and other controlled sources
www.fsc.org Cert no. SW-COC-002283
© 1996 Forest Stewardship Council
FSC

Printed on 100% post-consumer recycled paper

Publisher's Cataloging-In-Publication Data

Megre, V. (Vladimir), 1950-
    [Prostranstvo lʹiʹubvi. English.]
    The space of love / Vladimir Megré ; translated from the Russian by John
Woodsworth ; edited by Leonid Sharashkin. — 2nd ed., rev.

    p. : ill. ; cm. — (The ringing cedars series ; bk. 3)

    ISBN: 978-0-9801812-2-7

    1. Spirituality. 2. Nature—Religious aspects. 3. Human ecology. I.
Woodsworth, John, 1944- II. Sharashkin, Leonid. III. Title. IV. Title:
Prostranstvo lʹiʹubvi. English. V. Series: Megre, V. (Vladimir), 1950-
Ringing cedars series, bk. 3.

GF80 .M44 2008c
304.2   2008923348

Contents

CHAPTER ONE

Just another pilgrim

There she is! Again before mine eyes flows that mighty Siberian River, the Ob. I had finally reached the settlement where regular passenger service stopped, and was standing on the riverbank. In order to continue my journey to the spot where I could begin my trek through the taiga to Anastasia's glade, I would have to hire a small motorboat. Beside one of the many boats tied up along the shore three men were laying out some fishing tackle. I said hello to them and mentioned I was ready to pay good money for transport to such-and-such a place along the Ob.

"That's Yegorych's department. He charges a half-million roubles[1] for the trip there," answered one of the men.

I was concerned right off when I heard that someone here was already making passenger runs to the tiny Siberian village hidden way up north in the taiga. It was only twenty-five kilometres from there to Anastasia's glade. And the prices they were charging! It meant there must be takers. Demand creates a price like that. However, bargaining was something one did not do in the North, and so I asked:

"And where do I find this Yegorych?"

"He's somewhere in the settlement. Most likely at the store. See over there where the little tykes are playing — that's his boat. His grandson Vasya's with them. He'll run and fetch him — go ask him."

[1] *a half-million roubles* — approx. US$100 at the then current exchange rate — an exceptionally high price, roughly equivalent to an average Russian's monthly income.

No sooner had I greeted Vasya, a bright-looking lad of twelve or thereabouts, than he started rattling off:

"So, you need to go there? To see Anastasia? Wait just a moment! I'll go call my gramps in a sec!"

Without waiting for an answer, Vasya went dashing off to the settlement. I realised quite clearly he didn't need an answer. It was apparent that any strangers in these parts, in Vasya's opinion, had but one goal in mind.

I made myself as comfortable as I could by the riverbank and began to wait. There being nothing else to do, I stared at the water and drifted into thought.

The River was a good kilometre across at this point. Here amidst the boundless taiga (which you couldn't see the whole of even from an airplane), the River had been flowing on down through the centuries. What had it carried away of the past without leaving so much as a trace? What do these Ob waters remember from those times? Perhaps they remember how Yermak,[2] the 'conqueror of Siberia', pressed by his foes with his back against the River Ob, single-handedly tried to repel an enemy attack, and how his blood from a fatal wound seeped into the River, which then carried off his enervated body to goodness-knows-where... What did Yermak in fact conquer? Perhaps his deeds weren't that much different from the racketeering that goes on in modern times. Probably it is only the River that is in a position to judge today.

Or perhaps of greater importance to the River may have been the raids of Genghis Khan's troops? In ancient times his Horde was considered great indeed. There is a regional centre near Novosibirsk today known as Ordynskoe, which

---

[2]*Yermak* (a.k.a. Yermolai Timofeevich, 1540?–1585) — a Cossack *ataman* (chieftain), credited with heroic exploits in his campaign to open up the Siberian wilderness to Russian civilisation. In early August 1585 he was killed in a battle against the Tatar Khan Kuchum on the River Ob.

includes a village called Genghis. Perhaps the River remembers how Genghis' hordes retreated with their plundered booty, how they seized a young Siberian maiden, while a mighty vizier, starry-eyed with love, eloquently begged her to go with him of her own free will, with no resistance. The maiden remained silent, her eyes lowered. All the soldiers under the vizier's command had already fled, while he stayed and kept courting her with loving words. Finally he tossed her up onto the back of his steed along with a bag of gold, leapt into the saddle and made full speed for the banks of the Ob to escape his pursuers.

They began to catch up to him. The vizier started throwing the gold at them, and when the bag was empty he began tearing off his precious medals he had been awarded for conquering various lands and throwing them on the ground under his pursuers' feet, but he did not relinquish the maiden. With frothing mane the steed carried him to the canoes at the shore of the Ob. The vizier carefully helped the maiden down from his steed and seated her in one of the boats. Then he jumped in himself. But as he was poling the boat away from the shore he was pierced by an arrow from the pursuing forces right behind them.

The current began to carry the boat downstream. The wounded vizier lay near the stern, not even aware of the three large rowing canoes filled with soldiers coming ever closer. He looked tenderly at the maiden sitting calmly and quietly beside him, and fell silent himself — he had no strength left to speak. And the maiden looked at him, and then, with a glance at the overtaking canoes, she smiled faintly at them (or maybe at something else), tore the ropes off her hands and threw them into the water. Then this young Siberian maiden took to the oars. And none of the pursuer's craft could catch up to the boat carrying her and the wounded vizier.

To what place and into what age did the River current carry them? And what might the muddied waters of the River be carrying off at this moment in their memory of us?

Perhaps, dear River, you consider our big cities to be important? A huge city, Novosibirsk,[3] stands on the banks of the Ob, closer to its source in the south. Can you feel its great size and majesty, dear River? Of course, there's no doubt you would have a great deal to tell about it — you would say it pours a lot of pollution into you so that your once life-giving waters are no longer drinkable. But what can we do about it — where are we going to channel the waste from all the factories? After all, we, unlike our forebears, are in the process of developing. We have a lot of scientists working in the multitude of academic centres around Novosibirsk. And if we don't channel our waste into you, we shan't survive ourselves. And so the stench has made it hard to breathe in the city, and in some districts the smell is so bad and nobody even knows what it's from. Try to make sense of all this, dear River. Do you know — the technology we have today?! Instead of noiseless canoes, it's diesel ships that are now plying your waters. Including, at one time, my own.

I wonder whether the River remembers me. How I sailed up and down it on my ship — the largest passenger vessel in our fleet. It wasn't new, of course, the ship, and at full speed all its diesel engines and propellers made such a roar that it was even hard to hear the music in the bar.

What does the River cherish in its memory as the most important thing? In times past I would watch its shores from the upper deck of my ship, from the windows of the bar at the stern, listening to Malinin's[4] songs and romances:

[3]*Novosibirsk* — with a population of a million and a half, Siberia's largest city and major industrial, cultural and academic centre. It began in the 1890s as a major hub at the point where the Trans-Siberian Railway crossed the mighty Ob.

I was going to the city upon a white steed
When a pub-mistress smiled at me sweetly indeed.
Having caught on the bridge the old miller's sly glance,
I remained the whole night with that mistress, entranced.

The people busy with their activities along the shore seemed at the time to me petty and insignificant. Now I was one of them.

Another thing I thought about was how to convince Anastasia not to prevent me from communicating with my son. The situation was a strange one indeed, the way it had turned out. All my life I dreamt of having a son. I pictured how I would play with him as a little tyke, and then how I would raise him. When my son grew up, he would be a great help to me. We'd be business partners.

Now I have a son. And even though he's not around, it's still a jolly thing to know that somewhere on Earth there's a human being as close to you as that, your own flesh and blood, someone you very much wanted.

Before leaving I took great delight in purchasing for my son all sorts of basic kiddie things. Anyway, I went and bought them, sure, but whether or not I'll be able to give them to him — well, that's still a question mark. If my son had been borne by an ordinary woman — it wouldn't matter whether she were a country or a city girl — it would all be so simple and straightforward. Any woman would be delighted that her child's father was concerned and really trying to provide him with everything he needed, and take part in his upbringing.

---

[4]*Alexander Nikolaevich Malinin* (1958–) — a popular Russian singer-song-writer from Sverdlovsk (now Ekaterinburg), a large industrial city in the Urals. Famous for his masterfully performed romances, in 1998 he was honoured with the title *People's artist of Russia*. The verse here is the first stanza of his song *Bely kon* (White Steed).

In fact, if he didn't do this voluntarily, a lot of women would be applying for alimony.

But Anastasia was a taiga recluse with her own views on life and her own understanding of values. Even before our son's birth she made it clear to me:

"He doesn't need any material goods in your sense of the term. He will have everything he needs right from the start. You have the desire to give our baby some sort of senseless trinkets, which he doesn't need at all. You are the one who needs them for your own self-satisfaction, so you can say: 'Look at how good and attentive I am!'"

Why on earth would she say something like that — "He doesn't need any material goods"? Come on, now! What can a parent give his newborn child, then? Especially a father? It's still too early to start raising a breast-feeding infant in a fatherly way. How then can I express my relationship to him? How can I show him I care for him? A mother can breast-feed her baby, it's easier for her, she's already doing something, but what can a father do? In civilised circumstances he can help around the house, fix things up, take financial care of his family. But Anastasia doesn't need anything like that. All she has is her glade in the taiga. Her 'household' takes care of itself and waits on her hand and foot, which means the boy will get the same treatment once he's seen as coming from her.

I wonder how much it would cost to buy that kind of service? Sure, one can purchase or get a long-term lease on a few hectares of land easy enough, but what price can you put on the love and loyalty of a she-wolf, a she-bear, bugs and an eagle? Maybe Anastasia doesn't need any of the accomplishments of our civilisation, but why should the child have to suffer for his mother's crazy world-view? The child can't even have normal toys! She sees everything her own way. "The child doesn't need senseless trinkets, they'll only do him harm, distract him from the truth," she says.

Maybe in what she says there is some sort of quirky exaggeration or even downright superstition. There must be some reason mankind has invented so many different toys for kids! But so as not to quarrel with Anastasia, I didn't buy him any rattles — instead I got him a kiddie's constructor set, where the label on the box reads: "Develops children's intellect". Along with a quantity of disposable diapers, which the whole world uses today. And I bought a whole lot of powdered baby food. I'm really amazed at how easy they've made it. You open the box and there's a hermetically sealed package of waterproof foil. You just take a pair of scissors, cut open the packet, pour the contents into warm water, stir and... presto, it's all ready. They've got all sorts of powders — buckwheat, rice and other cereal grains.

The box says it has all sorts of vitamin additives. I remember, back when my daughter Polina was really little, having to go every day to the 'children's kitchen',[5] and now all you need do is buy a bunch of boxes and you can feed your own child with no trouble whatsoever. You don't even have to heat it up. Just dissolve in water, and that's it. I knew Anastasia didn't boil herself any water, and so, before buying up a whole lot, I bought a single box and tried adding the contents to water at room temperature — and it worked. I tried tasting it. It tasted normal — hardly any flavour, because there was no salt, but likely that's the way it should be for kids.

I decided Anastasia wouldn't be able to come up with any arguments against this powder. It would be silly to say no to a convenience like that. And that means she'll have to start showing a little respect to our technocratic world. It doesn't just produce weapons, it thinks about children too.

[5]*'children's kitchen'* (Russian: *domovaya kukhnia*) — a government-subsidised community canteen where parents (particularly mothers who were not breast-feeding) could go to get fresh dairy products, specially prepared for infants and young children.

But the thing that disturbed me most about what Anastasia said, especially since it didn't seem to make any sense, was this: she said that in order for me to communicate with my son, I would have to achieve a certain purity of thought, i.e., cleanse my inner parts. Only it wasn't clear to me just *what* inner parts I should cleanse.

It would have been understandable if she'd said I should shave, or shouldn't smoke, when I visited the child, or I should wear clean clothing. But she goes and talks on and on about conscious awareness and inner purging. And just where do they sell the brush that I can purge anything *there* with? Anyway, what have I got inside me that's so dirty? Maybe I'm not better than others, but I'm no worse either. Hey, if every woman started making a demand like that on her man, you'd have to set up a bloody purgatory for all mankind! It's... it's illegitimate, that's what it is!

I brought along a clipping from the civil code, where it says that one parent has no right to deprive the other of seeing their child without due cause, even if the parents are divorced. Of course, our laws don't mean very much to Anastasia, but still, it's a pretty strong argument. After all, the majority of people do observe the law. I ought to be able to take a hard line with Anastasia, too. We should have equal rights to our child.

I had thought earlier of taking a harder line with her. But now I've had some doubts about my initial decision, and here's why. Along with everything else in my backpack, I had brought along some letters from readers. I didn't bring them all, because I keep getting so many. I wouldn't begin to have room for them all. Many of the readers care a great deal about Anastasia. They call her a messiah, a fairy of the taiga, a goddess; they dedicate songs and poems to her. And some of them address her as though she were their bosom friend. This flood of letters got me reconsidering my words and actions in respect to Anastasia.

I had about a three-hour wait sitting beside Yegorych's boat. It was already late in the afternoon when I saw two men approach in the company of Yegorych's grandson. The first was getting on in years, he looked to be at least sixty. He wore a cloth raincoat and rubber boots. He was red in the face, obviously tipsy, since he staggered slightly as he walked. The second was younger, around thirty, and had a strong build. As they came closer, I noticed streaks of grey in the younger Siberian's dark-blond hair. The elder of the two came up to me and said:

"Hello there, traveller! So, you're off to see Anastasia? We'll take you. It'll be five hundr'd thousand for the trip plus two bottles[6] surcharge."

It was already clear to me that I wasn't the only one trying to reach Anastasia. That was why the price was so high. To them I was just another pilgrim on my way to Anastasia's habitat. But still I asked:

"How did you decide that I was going to see somebody named Anastasia, and not just to the village?"

"If you be goin' to the village or no, you'd better have the five hundr'd thousand ready. If you don't have the right amount, we won't take you there."

Yegorych's tone toward me wasn't exactly friendly.

They charge so much for the trip and yet don't talk very friendly, I thought. Why would that be?

Still, there was no alternative, and I had to accept the terms. But instead of being happy at all that money, and especially the two bottles of vodka he sent his young assistant to buy at the settlement, his attitude toward me only hardened. He sat down beside me on a rock and kept muttering to himself:

---

[6]*two bottles* — i.e., of vodka.

"To the village — what village? Six houses with people just barely alive — you call that a village? Who needs a village like that?"

"And do you often take visitors to see Anastasia? I'll bet you earn a pretty penny transporting them, eh?" I asked Yegorych, mostly to get a conversation going and soften his enmity. But Yegorych only answered in irritation:

"And who invited them to visit? We've got too many un-invited jerks barging in here. Nothing stops them. Did she invite them? Did she? No, she bloody well didn't! She told one bloke about her life. He goes and writes a book. Fine, write a book. But why give the location away? *We* never did. And here he meets with her once, and writes about her life, and gives the place away. That's something even females can understand: if you give it away, that's the end of her peace and quiet."

"Does that mean you've read the book about Anastasia?"

"I don't read books. Sashka,[7] my workmate here, he's a real bookworm. Anyway, we can't get you to the village tonight. Too far. The motor on the boat's not too strong. We'll make it as far as a fisherman's hut, spend the night there. Tomorrow Sashka'll take you on, while I do a bit of fishing."

"All right," I agreed, thinking it was just as well Yegorych had no idea I was the one who wrote about Anastasia.

Sashka, Yegorych's assistant, arrived with the vodka. Then they put the fishing tackle into the boat, at which point Yegorych's grandson Vasya all but cut the trip short. He started asking Yegorych for money to buy a new radio receiver.

"I've already fixed up a pole with an antenna — I've figured out how to set it up," said Vasya. "And I've got the antenna wire already. All you have to do is plug the antenna into the receiver and you pick up a whole bunch of stations right off."

---

[7] *Sashka* — like *Sasha*, a diminutive of *Alexander.*

CHAPTER TWO

Money for crap?

"You see what a bright lad I have for a grandson!" Yegorych proudly declared with a warmth in his voice. "A healthy curiosity, a budding craftsman! Way to go, Vasya! We'd better give him some money."

The hint was all too clear, and I started to pull out my wallet. But Vasya, encouraged by the words of praise, went on:

"I gotta listen to everything about the cosmonauts. Ours and the Americans'. When I grow up, I'm gonna be a cosmonaut."

"What?! What's that you said?!" Yegorych suddenly pricked up his ears.

"When I grow up, I'm gonna be a cosmonaut."

"The hell you are, Vasya! You're not gettin' any money from me for that kind of crap!"

"That ain't crap, no way, being a cosmonaut. Everybody likes cosmonauts. They're heroes, they show them on TV. They're always orbiting the Earth on their huge spaceships. They can talk with a whole lot of scientists right from space."

"And what good does all that chatter do? They're flying away up there, and in the meantime there's less and less fish in the Ob."

"The cosmonauts can tell everybody about the weather. They know ahead of everyone else what the weather will be like tomorrow anywhere in the world!" Vasya continued his defence of modern science.

"So what else is new? You go see Babka Martha.[1] Just ask Babka Martha and she'll tell you what the weather will be

tomorrow and the day after and next year. She won't charge
any money, not like your cosmonauts, eh? Those cosmonauts
of yours are wasting Petya's[2] money. Your father's money."

"The cosmonauts get a lot of money from the state."

"And where d'ya think the state gets its money from? From
where, dammit? It's from Petya, your father, that the state
gets its money. I catch some fish and Petya later sells it in
town. He wants to become this smart businessman, see, and
the state tells him: 'Pay your taxes, give us all your money —
after all, you know, we've got a lot of expenses.' And over in
the Duma[3] they just keep on fussin' and fussin', worse than a
bunch of old biddies at a well. The way they've over-invented
everything, they think they're the cat's whiskers! They've got
all sorts of amenities, their own, clean bathrooms to go to,
those smart asses, and meanwhile our river here gets dirtier
and dirtier. You're not gonna get any money, Vasya, 'til you
wash that nonsense of yours right out of your head. An' I
won't make any more trips, I'm not gonna earn good money
for crap like that."

Yegorych, probably because of his drunken state, got so
angry he was just about ready to cancel the trip. Then he un-
corked one of the vodkas Sashka had just brought from the
settlement and took a drink straight from the bottle. After
lighting a cigarette, he managed to calm down a bit, and we all
climbed into the boat. So he ended up not giving Vasya any
money and, instead, kept muttering something into his beard
about 'crap' during the whole trip.

---

[1] *Babka Martha* — the word *babka* in this sense refers to the local 'shaman'
of the village, an old woman held to be knowledgeable in folk medicine
and weather predictions.

[2] *Petya* — diminutive from *Petr* (pronounced *PYOTR*), the Russian equivalent of the name *Peter.*

[3] *Duma* — the national parliament of Russia.

The ageing motor sputtered noisily along. It was hard to make conversation above the din. We scarcely said a word until we reached an old hunter's hut with a single little window. The first stars appeared in the night sky. Having finished off en route the bottle he had begun at the point of departure, Yegorych muttered to his Sashka:

"I'm-m off to sleep. You make yourself comfy here by the fire or on the floor of the hut. When it gets light, take him to our spot."

Yegorych was already bending over to get through the tiny door of the hut, but all at once he turned around and repeated with an admonishing tone:

"To *our spot*! G-got it, Sashka?"

"Got it," Sashka calmly replied.

As we sat by the fire eating fish cooked over the coals, I asked Sashka a question about a phrase Yegorych had used which rather alarmed me.

"Alexander, can you tell me what this 'spot' of yours is where Yegorych told you to take me?"

"*Our* spot — that's on the opposite bank of the river from the village where you set out for Anastasia's glade," Alexander calmly replied.

"So *that's* it!" I exclaimed. "Here you go charging all this money, and you don't even take people where they need to go!"

"You're right, that's the way we do things. It's about all we *can* do for Anastasia, to make up for what we've done to her in the past."

"What have you done to her? And why are you confessing this to me? How can you take me to 'your spot' now?"

"I'll tie up the boat wherever you tell me to. As far as the money goes, I'll give you back my portion of it."

"So why do me a favour?"

"I recognised you. I recognised you right off, Vladimir Megré. I read your book and saw your photo on the cover.

I'll take you wherever you want. Only there's something I gotta tell you... You've got to listen calmly to what I say. An' think about it. You mustn't go into the taiga. You won't make it... Anastasia's gone. I think she's gone way back into some remote part. Or somewhere else — off into the unknown. You won't make it any more. You'll get yourself killed on the way. Or the hunters'll shoot you. The hunters won't tolerate any intruders on their lands. Intruders they deal with at a distance, so as not to subject themselves to unnecessary danger."

Alexander was outwardly calm as he spoke, only the stick he was stirring the embers with betrayed an awkward trembling, and the sparks flew up alarmingly into the night, like fireworks.

"Did something happen here? What was it? You recognised me, so tell me, what happened? Why did Anastasia go away?"

"I've been wanting to tell this myself," replied Alexander in a hushed voice. "I've been wanting to tell it to someone who will be able to understand. I don't even know where to begin so's you'll make sense of it... so's *I'll* make sense of it."

"Tell it simply like it is."

"Simply? You know, it's true, it's all really quite simple. Only it's so simple it's terrifying. Just hear me out calmly, if you can — don't interrupt."

"I'm not interrupting. Give me the gist of it. Don't drag it out."

Chapter Three

Uninvited guests

Alexander began speaking quietly, the way Siberian people do, and yet at the same time there was no mistaking the feeling of inner tension in the heart of this young Siberian fellow already showing streaks of grey in his hair.

"When I read your book *Anastasia,* I was a post-graduate student at Moscow University. I was interested in philosophy and psychology. I studied Oriental religions, and was really immersed in my studies. And then along came Anastasia. Not in some far-away land, but right in my own neighbourhood — Siberia, where I was born. And I could feel the tremendous power, logic and significance in her words! I could feel a kindred spirit — something that really spoke to me! The foreign theories I had been studying paled in comparison to the extraordinary feelings that now welled up in me. I dropped my studies and rushed home, as though from darkness to light. I really wanted to see Anastasia and talk with her.

"I came home and began making trips with Yegorych in the boat to the place you describe in your book. Yegorych and I figured out just where it was. From time to time other people would come and want to meet with Anastasia and ask about this spot. But we never took them there. The local residents had sense enough to realise what was happening and not give encouragement to the 'pilgrims'. But one time we — or, rather, I alone, without Yegorych — took a whole group of people to this place."

"Why did you do that?"

"At the time it seemed like I was doing the right thing, something good. It was a party of six. Two of them were prominent scholars and, from what I could tell, they had considerable resources at their disposal. Or those backing them, the ones who sent them, had considerable resources. The other four in the party were their security guards, armed with pistols, and something else besides. And they had two-way radios. I was invited to accompany them as their guide. I agreed, but not because of the money.

"I had a long talk with them first. They didn't conceal the goal of their expedition — a meeting with Anastasia. Their leader was a grey-haired, pleasant-looking chap named Boris Moiseevich.[1] He realised that Anastasia, all by herself, could do more for science than many research institutes.

"They planned to take her out of the taiga and set her up in a nature preserve where she could live under conditions she was accustomed to. And they'd guarantee her protection. Boris Moiseevich told me that if *they* didn't do this, someone else would. And anything might happen. Anastasia was an extraordinary phenomenon, and they felt obliged to protect her and study her.

"Boris Moiseevich had an assistant named Stanislav, a bright young man who claimed to be in love with Anastasia, even though he had never met her in person. I agreed with their arguments. They hired a small ship from a co-operative. They had a truck deliver barrels of aviation fuel to the ship.

"When we arrived at the spot, they set up tents on a promontory and summoned a helicopter on their two-way radio. The 'copter was outfitted for aerial photography; it also had a video camera and some other unusual equipment. Every day

---

[1]*Boris Moiseevich* — Here *Moiseevich* is a patronymic (derived from Boris' father Moisei), and not a surname. The use of his patronymic here, in contrast to Stanislav's first name used alone, indicates his position of seniority.

the helicopter would fly low over the taiga and take pictures, one quadrant after another.

"The two scientists made a daily examination of the pictures taken from the air. Occasionally they would travel on the helicopter themselves to a spot that interested them. They were looking for Anastasia's glade, where they planned to land the 'copter. I could only imagine the noise the 'copter would make landing in Anastasia's glade, scaring all the living creatures around. I remembered Anastasia had a baby and thought the roar from the 'copter might frighten him too.

"I tried to persuade the scientists that after determining the location of the glade they shouldn't set the 'copter down there. I proposed that once they determined the location they should draw up a map and go to the glade on foot. But Stanislav explained that Boris Moiseevich would find it difficult making the long trek through the taiga. Stanislav shared my concerns about disturbing the peace of the taiga residents, but assured me that Boris Moiseevich would be able to calm down both Anastasia and her baby. It all came to a head on the fourth day."

"What came to a head?"

"It happened when the 'copter flew off on a routine filming-and-photography trip, and we were busy back at our base. One of the guards noticed a lone female figure approaching our camp from the direction of the taiga. He reported this to Boris Moiseevich. Soon the whole camp was watching the woman approach. She was wearing a light cardigan and a long skirt, and the kerchief on her head was tied in such a way so that it covered her forehead and neck.

"We were standing together in a group, with Boris Moiseevich and Stanislav out in front. The woman came up to us. There was no fear or embarrassment showing in her face. And her eyes... She had the most extraordinary eyes — they looked at us tenderly, with kindness. And we could feel a warmth from her gaze. It seemed as though she was looking not at our group as a whole but at each one of us individually. We were all overcome by a feeling of excitement we couldn't explain. It was as though we had forgotten about everything else and were simply drinking in this warmth, basking in it — the warmth radiating from those extraordinary eyes of hers. And nobody even invited her to sit down and rest from her journey.

"She was the first to speak. And with a calm and unusually tender voice she said:

"'Good afternoon, people.'

"And we stood there without uttering a word. Boris Moiseevich was the first to respond.

"'Hello,' he replied for all of us. 'Please tell us who you are.'

"'My name is Anastasia. I have come to you with a request. Please call off your helicopter. It is very harmful for these parts. You are looking for me. Here I am. I shall answer any of your questions I am able to.'

"'Yes, of course, we've been looking for you. Thank you for coming on your own. That takes care of so many problems,' Boris Moiseevich began. But he still didn't ask her to sit down, even though there was a table and folding chairs by the tent. Nor did he take Anastasia aside to talk with her privately. He too was most likely distracted by her unexpected appearance. He started in right away telling her about why we had come.

"'Yes, that's very good... You came to us on your own. It was you, in fact, we had come for. Don't worry, we'll call off the helicopter right away.'

"Boris Moiseevich at once ordered the senior guard to radio the 'copter pilot to return to base. The order was carried out immediately. Then he turned to Anastasia and began talking with her in a calmer and more even tone.

"'Anastasia, the helicopter's coming now. You will climb aboard along with our colleagues. You will show our colleagues the glade where you live with your son. The 'copter will set down wherever you indicate, and you can fetch your boy. We'll take the two of you to a nature preserve near Moscow. Everything there will be arranged just as you say. That's only right. Nobody will disturb you there. The preserve is under twenty-four-hour guard, which will be reinforced once you settle in there. Just occasionally, scientists will come and talk with you at a time convenient for you. These people will be thoroughly prepared. You will find them interesting to talk to. And they will be most interested in your views on certain natural and social phenomena, as well as in your philosophy.

"'If you like, we'll provide you with a worthy assistant. Someone who will be constantly at your side and can catch your inner meanings. In spite of his young years, he is already a prominent and talented scholar. Besides which he has fallen in love with you even before meeting you. The two of you, I think, will be worthy mates — you have the potential to become a fine, happy couple. He is worthy of you not only because of his scholarship but in his lifestyle too. Here he is.' And at this Boris Moiseevich turned in Stanislav's direction, and beckoned him over.

"'Come along, Stanislav, don't dawdle! Introduce yourself.'

"Stanislav came over and stood facing Anastasia. He looked a little embarrassed as he started speaking.

"'Well, it looks as though Boris Moiseevich has already proposed for me! I know this may seem a trifle unexpected for you, Anastasia, but I really am ready to ask for your hand. I am prepared to adopt your son and treat him as my own child. I am ready to help you in working out a host of problems, and I ask you to consider me a friend.'

"Stanislav made an elegant bow before Anastasia, then took her hand and kissed it. He presented a most handsome and elegant appearance. And if only Anastasia had changed her clothes, they would really have looked like a most worthy and attractive couple.

"Anastasia replied to Stanislav in a tender, serious tone:

"'I thank you for your kind attentions to me. Thank you for caring about me.' And then she added: 'If you really feel you are strong enough to share your love and make another person's life happier and more fulfilled, then remember — there may already be in your circle of women friends someone who is dissatisfied with her life, unhappy about something. Pay attention to her, love her, make her happy.'

"'But I want to love *you*, Anastasia.'

"'I am already happy with another. Do not waste your energies on me. There are women out there who need you more than I do.'

"Boris Moiseevich decided to come to Stanislav's aid.

"'That other — is he the one whom you met with, Anastasia? No doubt you mean Vladimir. He's a long way from being the best example of our society.'

"'Whatever you say about him, it will not change my feelings. I cannot control my feelings.'

"'But why did you choose Vladimir to meet with in the first place? He's hardly what you could call either religious or scholarly, or even someone who leads a normal lifestyle. He's just an ordinary businessman. How did you happen to fall in love with him in particular?'

"At some point I began to realise," Alexander went on, "that Boris Moiseevich, Stanislav and the rest of the group had one clearly defined goal — to seize Anastasia, to take her by any means possible and use her only in their own interests, against her will. And it didn't matter whose idea it was — their own or on orders from somebody higher up, they would try their hardest to carry out their plan. And nothing — not even the most persuasive arguments — would stop them.

"Perhaps Anastasia understood this, too. She could hardly be ignorant or unaware of their intentions. And still she continued treating the men standing before her as kind and decent people, even as friends. She spoke sincerely and forthrightly on the most sacred of topics, and it was her attitude and sincerity which restrained, or rather forestalled, violence. She was so ingenious at countering Boris Moiseevich's and Stanislav's attempts to cool her feelings toward you that she showed all their arguments against you to be patently absurd.

"People say a woman in love sees only the good in the one she loves, no matter what he does or who he may really be. But *her* arguments were of quite a different sort. After the first flurry of excitement over Anastasia's appearance had passed, I was able to quietly switch on my tape recorder.

"Later I would often listen and analyse what Anastasia said. I remember it all. And that 'all' was enough to turn my whole consciousness upside down."

"What turned your consciousness upside down?" I queried, wondering what Anastasia had said about me. And Alexander went on:

"When Boris Moiseevich asked: 'How did you happen to fall in love with him in particular?', Anastasia countered with a simple, direct reply:

"'There is no point in asking me a question like that. Nobody who is in love can explain why they love the person they do. For every woman in love there will be only one man who is the best and most significant person in the world — and that is the one she has chosen. And my beloved is the very best one for me.'

"'But still, Anastasia, you cannot fail to grasp the absurdity of your choice. Even if it happened spontaneously, it's still absurd. That first breath of passion should have been chilled by your will, your abilities, the logic of your mind. They should have shown you how unworthy this man was compared to others. Think about it, carefully.'

"'When I think about it carefully I come to exactly the opposite conclusion. In this case any further reflection is a waste of time. It only adds to the mysterious inevitability of what took place. Better just accept everything as it is.'

"'What, accept an absurdity? A paradox?'

"'It only seems to be that way at first glance. You have made a long trip here from Moscow. You had quite a challenge getting to that spot on the riverbank. You ask questions about my love. But you do not seem to have grasped hold of another paradox — namely that this love can be better and more clearly explained by events that happened in Moscow. And it would have been better for you to reflect on them right there. It would have saved you coming all this way.'

"'What kind of events happened in Moscow?'

"'On the surface they are very simple. But only on the surface. Right after meeting with me, Vladimir, whom you call a simpleton, an unremarkable and even malicious person, abandoned everything and left Siberia to go to Moscow. He went there to keep his word to me — to organise a fellowship of purer-minded entrepreneurs. Even though he had no money left, he still acted.

"'In Moscow there is a two-storey building at 14 Tokmakov Lane. That is where the people used to work who were in charge of the first association of entrepreneurs. Then the people in charge left and the association started to fall apart.

"'Vladimir went in there and things started to pick up again in its empty offices, both the large and small ones. There he wrote various letters addressed to entrepreneurs. He worked in his office from early morning until late at night and even stayed there to sleep. People would come and see him or just turn up and start helping him. They believed in him and what he was doing. I asked him to do this when he was with me in my glade here in the taiga. I told him how important it was.

"'I worked out a plan of action and presented it to him. The goals were achievable, provided he carried out the plan in the order that had come to me in my dream. He was supposed to write the book first. And then use the book to explain a lot of things and spread information. It was the book that was to have found and brought together pure-minded entrepreneurs. And provide him with the funds for carrying out this plan.

"'But Vladimir did everything the right way as *he* saw it. He hardly thought of me at all. He realised the significance of the plan and put it into practice. Only he did it *his* way, and changed the sequence.

"'That way the goal was unachievable. He did not know this, and he acted with incredible persistence and resourcefulness. Other people who believed in the idea started helping him. The new entrepreneurs' association very slowly began to sprout and grow in size. It was incredible, but things started moving just a wee bit. They were getting together. And these were pure-minded entrepreneurs. There is a list of their names and addresses — you can go check yourselves.'

"'We looked at this list. It was published in the first edition of the book. But I'm sorry to have to disappoint you, Anastasia. It will be a disappointment! The list included such enterprises as *Kristall,* a Moscow distillery. Its product is incompatible with any concept of the divine.'

"'Everything in the world is relative. And perhaps this *Kristall* is not so bad in comparison with some others. Besides, we are talking about thoughts pure enough to change *everything.* Today's reality is the result of yesterday's thinking.'

"'I can agree with what you are saying there. Still, your Vladimir failed to organise a fellowship of pure-minded entrepreneurs. I assure you, Anastasia, you've pinned your hopes on the wrong man.'

"'After changing the sequence of events, Vladimir was unable to reach his goal. He did not have even the slightest opportunity or any funds to circulate information beyond Moscow. He came up against adverse circumstances and he lost the offices where he could have continued his work, he lost his means of communication as well as his sleeping quarters. He left the building in Tokmakov Lane, along with the little group of local people who were helping him. He could not afford to pay his assistants for their work. He left without a kopeck to his name. He had no place to live and not even any winter clothing. He had forsaken his family and been forsaken by his family. And do you know what he talked about with his little group of helpers as they headed for the metro along the icy streets? He talked about starting everything again from scratch. Even under those conditions he was working out a plan, trying to get something going. After all, he is an entrepreneur. They, his helpers, followed him; they listened to him and believed him. They loved him.'

"'What for, if I may ask?'

"'You go ask them, these Moscow people, what for — ask *them* what they found in him. Go to the building on Tokmakov Lane and ask the security guards there why each time they came on duty they would bring him some food in jars or wrapped in cloth, to give him a decent supper. They tried to do it in such a way so as not to offend him with their charity. These burly security guards, who did not have to answer to him, cooked borshch and other kinds of soup at home and brought it to him so he could have something of a homemade meal. They loved him. Why?

"'When you visit that building, go have a talk with the pretty woman who used to work as a secretary there. She is a former actress, she played the lead as the kind alien-girl in the film *Cherez ternii k zvyozdam* (Through the thorns to the stars).[2] She played her very well. It was a good film, calling upon people to care for and love the Earth. Ask her why she, an employee of another firm in the same building, tried to help Vladimir inconspicuously — and she did help him. She was not *his* secretary, but she helped him. Why did she endeavour to bring my beloved coffee or tea for his lunch? She made it look as though it were her firm which was supplying her with the sugar, tea and biscuits. In fact she brought everything from her own home. She was not rich. She loved him. Why?

"'At the same time he, Vladimir, was still losing his strength, he was dying. He was physically exhausted. But even on death's doorstep he kept trying to reach his goal. He is an entrepreneur, after all. And his spirit is strong.'

"'Anastasia, you're talking in metaphors. What do you mean when you say he was dying? In an allegorical sense?'"

"'In a literal sense. When he was in Moscow, his flesh was just about dead for several days in a row. People in such a condition usually lie motionless. But he was up and about.'

"'Possibly thanks to *you*, Anastasia?'

"'All during those forty-two terrible hours I never ceased warming him with my ray, not even for a moment. But it was not enough. My ray could not retain life in a body if the spirit were weakening. But Vladimir's spirit was fighting back. In its struggles his spirit did not notice death approaching. It helped the ray. Then other little rays came to the aid of my ray. They were altogether weak and unconscious, but they were there. These were the rays of those around Vladimir in Moscow — people who loved him.

[2] *Through the thorns to the stars* — a 1980 Russian science-fiction film, directed by Richard Viktorov, starring Yelena Metyolkina as the cloned alien Niya from the planet Dessa, rescued from a stranded alien spaceship by Russian cosmonauts.

"'His practically dead flesh began to be filled with life. When confronted by sincere love, if it is strong enough, death retreats. The immortality of Man[3] is in love, in his ability to ignite love within himself.'[4]

"'I say, Anastasia: dead flesh can't walk about. You're still speaking in allegories, not scientifically.'

"'The criteria of human science are always temporary. There are truths that are valid beyond the present moment.'

"'But how then can modern scientists be convinced? We need results from objective measuring devices.'

"'Fine. Go to the Kursk Terminal.[5] There's an automatic photo booth in one of the adjacent metro stations. During that bad period Vladimir had his picture taken for an I.D. card — one of those small colour prints. You may still be able to find it at the building at 42 Leninsky Prospekt. Or Vladimir himself might have it. Take a careful look, and you will see all the outward signs of a dead body; the automatic camera captured even the death spots on his face. But you will also see life in his eyes. And a fighting spirit.'

"'And yet you were the only one who could rescue him, Anastasia. Tell me how it is that you ended up spending so much of your energies on *him*? Why?'

"'I was not the only one who came to his rescue. Ask the three Moscow students why they rented an apartment for him at their own expense? When he finally realised the reason

[3]*Man* — Throughout the Ringing Cedars Series, the word *Man* with a capital *M* is used as the equivalent of the Russian word *chelovek*, including both male and female, as, for example, the word *man* is used in Genesis 1: 27 (see Translator's Preface to Book 1).

[4]*within himself* — it is possible that 'toward himself [on the part of others]' may be intended in the original.

[5]*Kursk Terminal* — one of the major railway terminals in central Moscow — a modern structure with a glass façade, constructed in 1972. It is connected to three different metro (subway) stations.

he was failing and set about writing the book, why did they, right in the middle of an exam period and trying to earn more money wherever they could, spend their evenings keyboarding Vladimir's text into their computers? Why? You can ask the same question of many Moscow residents who were at Vladimir's side in his times of need. The solution to the mystery lies in them, not in me. Why did Moscow and her people help him and take care of him, why did they believe in him?

"'The city of Moscow was also writing the book. I am thrilled with that city! I have fallen in love with it! No amount of roaring machines or senseless cataclysms devised by the technocratic world can nullify the embrace of kindness and love from the hearts of its people. Many, many residents of this city are reaching out for kindness and brightness — for love. Through all the bustle and the clamour of roaring machinery they feel its tremendous power and grace.'

"'But, Anastasia, what you say is really incredible and overwhelming. It couldn't happen all by itself. Once again it shows the incredible scope of your abilities, the extraordinary possibilities of that ray you possess. You have evidently used it to enlighten the Moscow people who got in touch with Vladimir. You won't deny, now, that you did that? And that you were the one who made all these miracles happen!'

"'Love is what makes miracles happen. And I did use my ray to make careful contact with all those in communication with Vladimir. But all I did was to give a bit of strengthening to the feelings of goodness, love and bright aspirations that they already had. I only strengthened what was in them already.

"'And the book was published by Moscow. The first print-run was small and it was a pretty slim volume. But people started buying it. It quickly sold out. Far from distorting the events he had witnessed in the taiga, it honestly described the feelings he had experienced. In the eyes of many readers I came out looking clever and good, while Vladimir appeared stupid and none too bright.

"'People in their homes reading the book did not take into account that Vladimir was with me one on one in the remote Siberian taiga. Everything back then was still extremely un- familiar to him. And I do not know who else could go so far into the taiga with no gear at all. Or how such a person would behave upon seeing what Vladimir saw. Vladimir was honest in the way he depicted everything. And yet for many people he began to look stupid. And here you are asking me: *Why did I choose him? And why do I love him so?*

"'In the process of writing the book, Vladimir was already turning his thinking around on a great many things. He grasps everything very quickly. Anyone who has the opportunity of talking with him cannot fail to notice that. But he never tried to paint a rosy picture of his former self.'"

CHAPTER FOUR

Chords of the Universe

"Anastasia spoke warmly about you," Alexander continued. "She knew all about people and events. She told them that the first book you wrote came out in Moscow in a small print-run, and it immediately led to enthusiastic reviews, poetry, paintings and songs. She said that thanks to the sincerity of the writing, the book preserved the combinations and symbols she had sought out in the Universe, and these were what aroused the extraordinary beneficial, panacean feelings in people.

"When Boris Moiseevich heard that, he began fidgeting, and abruptly sat down at the table by the tent. I noticed he was surreptitiously trying to switch on a tape recorder. He was probably so caught up with the pursuit of important information that he completely forgot about everyone else around. He didn't even offer Anastasia a chair, he was so bent on extracting as much information from her as he could, and quickly. This old grey-haired fellow was excited and fired off more questions:

"'Scientists in many countries of the world are trying to capture the extraordinary sounds of the Universe with their costly specialised equipment. These sounds are out there. They are known to science. Maybe not all of them, just a few for the time being. Maybe just a billionth part of the whole. What devices do you use to capture them, Anastasia? What equipment will allow us to select the sounds that can exert an effective influence on the human mind?'

"'The equipment one needs has existed for a long time already. It is called the human soul. The attitude and purity of the soul will accept or reject sounds from the Universe.'

"'Okay, fine. Okay. Let's assume. Let's assume you've managed to... to find and select from the billions of sounds the best that the Universe has to offer, and then recombine them in the right way. But sound can only be reproduced with the help of a device or a particular musical instrument. What's the point of a book, then? After all, it can't make sounds.'

"'You are right, a book does not make sounds. But it can serve as a score, like a musical score. The reader will involuntarily utter within himself any sounds he reads. Thus the hidden combinations in the text will resonate in the reader's soul in their pristine form, with no distortion. They are bearers of Truth and healing. And they will fill the soul with inspiration. No artificial instrument is capable of reproducing what resonates in the soul.'

"'How did Vladimir manage to preserve all your combinations if he himself knew nothing about them?'

"'I took note of Vladimir's speech patterns. Besides, I knew in advance that Vladimir would not distort the essence of the events or what he heard, that he would even present himself just the way he was. But he did not convey all the combinations of signs. He needed to carry on writing. After all, he set forth only a fraction of what he knew and was trying to make sense of when he started to write. He needed to continue with the writing.

"'And he has already been touched by fame. An unprecedented fame at that. It would have taken only a little more effort to organise the fellowship of entrepreneurs. But then all of a sudden he took another step my dream did not anticipate. He left his Moscow apartment — on which the rent was already paid — to his Moscow entourage, he left to them the privilege of receiving compliments from readers, while he himself boarded a train and headed out of town.'

"'Why did he do that?'

"'He had been wanting all along to seek out confirmation of some of the things I had said — scientific confirmation of the existence of various phenomena I had talked about. To investigate them. That is why he decided not to write any more for the time being. And so he went off to the Caucasus. He left Moscow to see the dolmens in the Caucasus with his own eyes — the ancient structures where living people went to die ten thousand years ago. I had told him about them. I also told him about the important functional significance these dolmens have for people living today.

"'Vladimir came to the city known as Gelendzhik. In the museum there, along with museums in Krasnodar and Novorossiysk, he collected material on the dolmens.[1] Then he met with various scientists, archæologists and local ethnographers who were studying the dolmens. He ended up with considerably more information on them than was available in any one museum.

"'Naturally I tried to help him inconspicuously. I used the mouths of people who came to see Vladimir to inculcate a good deal of new information in him, so that he would have the opportunity to make his conclusions. But he also did his part by acting quickly and decisively. This was after he had compared all the information he had gathered with what I had told him, after the archæologists had shown him the dolmen closest to the road and he discovered that there were others, but that they had fallen into ruin for lack of proper attention from the local residents. The local people had never been much interested in them.

"'Vladimir then did something that might seem incredible. In three months he managed to change the attitude of the local residents toward the dolmens. They began bringing flowers. The women ethnographers of the Gelendzhik museum

---

[1]*Gelendzhik, Krasnodar, Novorossiysk, dolmens* — See footnotes 1 and 2 in Book 1, Chapter 30: "Author's message to readers", as well as Book 2, Chapter 1: "Alien or Man?".

set up a public association, which they called "Anastasia" in my honour. This association opened a school for tour-guides in order to get the right message out to tourists about the dolmens, so they would preserve and take care of the dolmens instead of destroying them. In addition, they began organising new tours, which they called "Excursions into reason".[2]

"'The tour-guides at Gelendzhik began telling everyone about the significance of our pristine origins and about the works of the Grand Creator — about Nature.'

"'Anastasia, do you think this was all because of him? Didn't you play a part here?'

"'If I could have done as much as this without him, I would have done it long ago. I very much wanted to. It is in one of the distant dolmens in these mountains that my foremother's flesh approached its death.'

"'But how? How did one man, a nobody, manage to change people's attitudes in so short a time? And how could he have set up such an active association? You say that the local residents had access to scientific materials and all sorts of publications, since people knew about them at the museums. But they didn't pay any attention.'

"'That is correct: they knew about them but did not pay attention.'

"'But why did they then listen to *him*? How did he manage to pull it off? You can't change people's consciousness *that* quickly.'

"'But Vladimir did not know that. He did not know that consciousness cannot be changed quickly, and that is why he acted and, in fact, changed it. Go visit that city, ask the different people who joined this association. Find out how and why fortune smiled on Vladimir.

---

[2]According to the Association's leader, Valentina Larionova, in the years since the organisation was established in 1996, over half a million visitors have visited the dolmens through this Association alone; the total number is much higher.

"'I was thrilled by what was happening there. The "Anastasia Association". He agreed to the name when they asked him about it. I thought he did it for me, that he was beginning to understand me and love me. And he really has managed to grasp a great deal, but he has not fallen in love with me. He has not done so because of my many mistakes and transgressions.

"'I soon began to figure this out. I began to realise that my dream was actually coming true. And that people would indeed be transported across the dark forces' window of time. And that people would be happy! What I dreamt about would come true, except that my love for him was not to be requited. And this was payment for the many mistakes I had made, my lack of perfection and my own insufficient purity of thought.'

"'What happened? What made you come to that conclusion?' Boris Moiseevich queried. 'In any case, everybody's known for a long time how coarse and uncivilised this fellow is. Believe me, Anastasia, as your senior and as the father of a family, I can tell you that your parents would not have approved of such a union.'

"'I beg you, do not talk that way about one who is so dear to me. Regardless of how coarse Vladimir may appear to some people, I know differently.'

"'What else is there to know about him? Everybody knows what kind of people entrepreneurs are,[3] and he's just a typical example of the species, that's clear to all. Anastasia, I must say you have a rather biassed opinion of Vladimir.'

"'No matter, it is still my opinion. Besides, your assumption regarding my parents' views is wrong.'"

---

[3]Partly because of so many years of communist indoctrination, *entrepreneurs* in 1990s Russia were stereotyped as having low moral and ethical standards, interested primarily in their own enrichment at the expense of ordinary citizens.

CHAPTER FIVE

The spirit of a foremother

"'I realised it one morning...' Anastasia said quietly, and her gaze looked as though it were immersing itself in the past, 'a morning when Vladimir was not at home in the flat he had rented temporarily. I could not find him with my ray. It was the morning of the day when my foremother went into a dolmen to die many centuries ago. I always think of her on that anniversary. I try to talk with her. And she talks with me. You people are accustomed as well to going to the cemetery on a day you remember your loved ones, to think about them, even talk with them. I can do this without leaving my glade. My ray helps me both see and talk at a distance, and they can feel my ray.

"'On that day I was thinking about my foremother, trying to talk with her as usual, but I could not sense any reply from her. None at all. She was not responding to me. This had never happened before. Then I tried to locate her dolmen with my ray. I found it. I shone my ray upon it with all my might. My foremother did not respond. Something had happened I did not know about. My foremother's spirit was not in the dolmen.'

"'Anastasia, please explain what you mean by someone's "spirit". What does it consist of?'

"'It consists of all the unseen elements in a Man, including certain passions and sensations acquired during the period of existence in the flesh.'

"'Does the spirit possess an energy, analogous to any of the energies we know of?'

"'That is correct. It is an energy complex, consisting of a multitude of different energies. After the end of a human individual's fleshly existence, certain of these complexes break up into separate energies, which are subsequently used in plant and animal aggregates, as well as in essential natural phenomena.'

"'What kind of power do they have? What is the energy potential of unbroken complexes?'

"'They vary from individual to individual. The weakest ones cannot even overcome gravitational energy — they will later fall apart, no matter what.'

"'Gravitational, you say? The weakest ones? Is it possible to see their presence in anything at all? To touch it? Feel it?'

"'Of course. In a tornado, for example.'

"'A tornado? You mean a tornado which rips trees up by the roots and overturns things? Then what kind of energy do the strongest ones have?'

"'The strongest? Well, that would be *Him*. I cannot fully fathom the strength of His energy.'

"'Then, let's say, somewhere in between, something average?'

"'The energy complex of many average spirits already contains a released mental energy.'

"'What would be the strength or energy potential of an average complex like this?'

"'I already told you: it contains released mental energy.'

"'What does that mean? What can it be compared to? How would you define it?'

"'To what can it be compared? A definition? Tell me, what is the most powerful energy that your mind, your thought or consciousness can imagine?'

"'The energy of a nuclear explosion. No, rather, the energy of the reactions taking place at the Sun's core.'

"'Everything you have named is equivalent to but a tiny fraction of released mental energy. As for definitions, those are things you think up yourselves to use in verbal communication with each other. Not a single definition you have ever thought of is applicable here. You can use the ones you are familiar with if you multiply them to the power of infinity.'

"'Tell me, what is the strength of your foremother's energy?'

"'It contains released mental energy.'

"'How did you find out about your foremother? How and where did she die? After all, that happened ten thousand years ago!'

"'That information — about my foremother who went into the dolmen to die — was passed down from generation to generation of her descendants.'

"'Did your mother tell you about her?'

"'I was only an infant when my mother perished. I was not capable of taking in that kind of information. My grandfather and great-grandfather told me all about my foremothers.'

"'Can her spirit be seen with normal human vision?'

"'Partially. If one changes one's spectral perception, along with one's inner rhythm.'

"'Is that possible?'

"'The phenomenon you know as *Daltonism*[1] suggests that it *is* possible. You believe it is something beyond the will of Man, that it is merely a disease, but that is not so.'

"'You said your ancestor, your foremother, was worthy enough to have information about her transmitted from generation to generation over the millennia? What makes this information so worthy, so valuable?'

---

[1]*Daltonism* — a red-green type of colour-blindness (also known as *deuteranopia* or *deuteranomaly*), named after English chemist and physicist John Dalton (1766–1814), who was also a teacher of mathematics and natural philosophy. His theory of colour-blindness was published in a paper entitled "Extraordinary facts relating to the vision of colours, with observation" (Manchester, 1798).

"'My foremother was the last from our pristine origins who knew what a woman should think about during the breast-feeding of an infant and had the ability to do so. Civilisation was gradually losing sight of the knowledge people had ten thousand years ago, and it has all but disappeared completely today. My foremother was by no means an old woman, but she went into the dolmen to die in order to preserve all this knowledge of our pristine origins. And when people's awareness begins to be restored, people will become aware of the need to transmit this knowledge to nursing mothers. And after that they will help each other learn everything. Through her death in the dolmen my foremother learnt even greater truths that women need to know.'

"'Why did she decide to go into a dolmen? How does a dolmen differ from the usual kind of stone tomb? And why did she not wait until she was old before going into the dolmen to die? Was she motivated by an awareness of her goal, or simply by superstition?'

"'Back then they had already begun paying less attention to the breast-feeding of infants and women were not offered the opportunity of entering a dolmen, even if they wished to. The ageing leader revered my foremother and comprehended that if *he* did not accede to her request, the leader-to-be would not listen to her at all, and her intentions he might well dismiss as mere fancy.

"'But the menfolk could not be compelled by their leader to build my foremother a dolmen, and so he gave her his own. The men did not approve of the leader's decision and refused to lift the stone slab covering the top so she could go in. So the women got together as one and all night long tried to lift the slab of heavy stone. The next morning at dawn the old leader came. He did not do much walking any more, yet still he came, leaning on a staff. The old leader smiled at the women, said some encouraging words, whereupon the heavy slab yielded to the women's upward thrust, and my foremother went in.'

"'And how does a dolmen differ from an ordinary stone tomb?'

"'There is not much difference outwardly. But the dolmen, as you call this stone tomb, was a place where *living* people went to die. The dolmen was not simply a religious structure, as people tend to think today. It is a monument to wisdom and the great self-sacrifice of one's spirit for the sake of future generations. Even today it has a significant functional purpose. And the death experienced in one of these dolmens was not an ordinary one. Actually, the word *death* is not all that appropriate here.'

"'I can imagine,' Boris Moiseevich said. 'A living person entombed in a stone chamber... That is really extraordinary — it must have been an extremely torturous death.'

"'The people who went into the dolmens did not suffer. The peculiarity of their death lay in the fact that they meditated. They meditated on eternity, and in spirit they would remain forever on the Earth, and even hold on to certain earthly feelings. But the soul of those who went into a dolmen to die was forever deprived of the possibility of material re-embodiment on the Earth.'

"'How did they meditate?'

"'You are aware today — especially from the ancient Oriental religions — of what meditation is. And there are teachings today that can help one become acquainted with a small fraction of the phenomena of meditation, but not, unfortunately, with its underlying purpose. And today there are people who are capable of meditating — temporarily separating part of their spirit from their body and then returning it to the body. Through the help of meditation in the dolmen, even while the body was still alive, the spirit completely separated itself and returned many times, while the flesh was still living. After that the spirit remained forever in the dolmen. All alone, it would eternally wait for visitors to impart to them the wisdom of our pristine origins. Even if the flesh succeeded in living a while longer, it was still cloistered. But while it was alive, the spirit had the freedom to travel back and forth between different dimensions, which afforded it the opportunity of analysing at incredible speed (according to your calculations) the truth that was available, as though clarifying the truth for itself.

"'One who died, or entered into eternal meditation through the dolmen, knew that his soul or spirit would never again be able to take on a material form. It would never again be able to embody itself in earthly flesh, or matter. It would never be able to go far from the dolmen or leave it for any length of time, but it would have the ability to communicate with a particle of the soul of a person living in the flesh who had come to visit the dolmen. And if you talk about a torturous death, about suffering in general, in this case the torture lies in the fact that for millennia now nobody has come to acquire this knowledge. The great tragedy of the dolmens is the utter lack of demand. That same demand for which —'

"'Anastasia,' Boris Moiseevich interrupted, 'how important do you feel it is for nursing mothers to have this knowledge and ability?'

"'Extremely important,' she replied.

"'But why? After, all, mother's milk feeds only the *flesh* of an infant.'

"'Not only the flesh. It is capable of transmitting a huge quantity of information, as well as a keen sensitivity. You must be aware, after all, that every substance includes its own kind of information, its own radiance and vibration.'

"'Yes, I know. But how can mother's milk transmit sensitivity?'

"'It can — it is extremely sensitive. It is inextricably linked to the feelings of the mother. The taste of the milk can change according to her feelings. And stress can even cause the milk to congeal or stop coming altogether.'

"'Yes, that can indeed happen. It can. And you say nobody comes to visit your foremother? That means nobody's come over many thousands of years?'

"'At first people came. Mainly the generations of relatives and people living there. After that a series of cataclysms began happening on the Earth. People began migrating. The dolmen remained where it was. But over the past millennia nobody has come to visit my foremother to find out... Now the dolmens are all being laid waste. Because people do not know.

"'In the taiga, when I first told Vladimir about the dolmens and my foremother, he said that perhaps he would go visit her dolmen. Then I explained how it was impossible for him to comprehend or feel my foremother's spirit and accept the information she had to give. Men simply do not know the feelings and sensations inherent in a nursing mother. All these millennia my foremother has been waiting for women, not men, to come see her. But no women have come to her dolmen. And I am the only one to communicate with her, once a year. And on that particular day I wanted to be in contact with her, and tell her something good. But I could not. My foremother's spirit was not anywhere close to the dolmen. I had no idea why, and began quickly searching with my ray all around, in a constantly widening radius. And then all at once: I found her! I found her! In a ravine among the rocks.

"'Vladimir was lying on the rocks unconscious. And my foremother, her spirit, was bending over Vladimir, taking form as a conglomeration of invisible energies. I realised then what had happened. I had known even earlier that Vladimir was looking for guides to take him to the dolmens located far away from the main road. But he could not find any. No one would volunteer to accompany him. And so Vladimir decided to go into the mountains alone. At one point he fell off the path into a ravine. He was wearing ordinary shoes — not suitable for mountain hiking. In fact, he did not have any mountain gear at all.

"'He wanted to be convinced that the dolmens really existed, he wanted to touch them. And so he went into the mountains alone. On my foremother's memorial day he went to the dolmens located far away from the road. My foremother did not know why this poorly equipped person had come into the mountains. And she kept her eye on him. And when he slipped and started falling, she suddenly... Like a supple mass of air her spirit swept down to his side.

"'My foremother saved Vladimir's life. While he did not actually strike his head on a rock, the many bruises he received in the fall caused him to lose consciousness. My foremother used her supple air mass to hold up his head, as though supporting it with her hands, and waited for him to regain consciousness. That was why she did not speak with me. Even when Vladimir's consciousness returned, she still did not go back to her dolmen. She remained in the ravine down below. She stayed to watch as Vladimir climbed back up to the path.

"'Later I realised that my foremother was actually on the path, since stones began rolling out of the way. That was her doing. She had taken on the form of a supple breeze, sweeping the stones away from the mountain path. She wanted to help Vladimir in his descent. I very much wanted to do the same. And so I began to ever so quickly move along the path with my ray, so that it wouldn't be so wet and slippery and Vladimir could get safely back to the place he was staying and treat his wounds.

"'Once Vladimir had climbed back up from the ravine, he sat down on the path and examined the sketch one of the archæologists at the Novorossiysk Museum had drawn for him. Then he got up and started walking, with a limp. But not downward, along the dry path that had now been cleared of stones, but the opposite way: upward. I was shocked at this unexpected turn of events, and I believe my foremother did not immediately grasp his intentions either. At this point he left the path altogether and clambered through a thicket of thorny bushes.

"'I realised he was trying to reach my foremother's dolmen. He succeeded. He sat down on the portico in front of the dolmen, at the edge of one of the stone slabs, and began unbuttoning his jacket. His arm hurt and it took him a long time. When his jacket was completely unbuttoned I could see he had a bouquet of flowers underneath. Three little roses. The stems of two of them were broken. The flowers had been damaged when he fell into the ravine and struck the rocks. Some of the thorns on the stems were blood-covered. He placed the damaged roses on the dolmen's portico and lit a cigarette. And then he said:

""'Too bad the flowers got smashed. These flowers are for you, my beauty. You must have been a real beauty, just like Anastasia. You were smart, and kind. You wanted to tell our women all about breast-feeding children. Only they have no idea you exist. And the fact that your dolmen is so far off the beaten path makes it difficult for women to get here."

"'Then Vladimir took out a shallow little flask of brandy and two little metal goblets, and pulled out a fistful of squashed candies from his pocket. He poured brandy into the goblets. He drank one of them, placed the other on the dolmen's portico, covering it with a piece of candy, and said: "This is for you, my beauty!"

"'Vladimir did everything people do today at cemeteries when they come to see their loved ones or dear friends. As for my foremother... Her spirit kept sweeping around him in the form of an invisible energy mass. She was distraught, and did not know what to do. She tried to show some kind of response to Vladimir's words, tried congealing the air into the shape of her body, but her outlines were transparent and barely noticeable. Vladimir did not notice them. He could not see or hear anything. She kept on trying her best to explain everything to him, but could only sweep back and forth in frustration.

"'At one point her air mass lightly touched the goblet sitting on the portico and overturned it. Vladimir thought a random gust of wind had done this, and joked:

"""Hey, what're you up to, my wayward friend — spilling expensive brandy like that?"

"'And my foremother's spirit fell still in a corner of the dolmen. Vladimir poured some more brandy, placed a little stone on top, and then put another piece of candy on top of that. And again he started talking, as though to himself:

"""We need to get a decent pathway in here. Just wait a bit. There will be a proper path to your dolmen. And that way women will come to see you. You will tell them everything they need to think about in breast-feeding an infant. Indeed, you must have had very beautiful breasts."

"'Then Vladimir started his descent. It was late at night when he got back to the place he was staying. He sat for a while alone on the sofa in his cold apartment, binding his wounds and watching a videocassette. Someone had given him a tape to watch which had been copied and passed around by people in various places.

"'On the tape there was a speaker in front of a large audience made up mainly of women. He was talking about God and how strong the spirit of a righteous Man could be. Then he started talking about me. He said I was an ideal woman — a role model to which people should aspire. He said that I had great strength of mind and spirit and that I was aided by the forces of Light, and that now, once I became familiar with the lives of people in the usual world, I would be able to help them.

"'He said a lot of nice things about me. And then, all at once... He said that I had not yet met a real man. And that the one I had been in contact with was not a real man. Indeed, others had been saying earlier that there was a young man in Australia who was worthy of me, that he and I would meet, and then I would meet a real man.

"'And Vladimir, he... You see — he was sitting all alone there, listening to this. All this time he was trying with one hand to bind the wounds on his legs. His other hand still hurt too much from the bruises. I reached out to Vladimir at once with my ray. I wanted to warm his wounds, and chase his pain away. And to tell him... Somehow tell him... Even though he never hears me when I speak to him at a distance, I thought, well, this time it might work out... Yes, I thought it might work out this time since my longing for him to hear me was so strong. I wanted him to hear how I loved him! Only him. And only *he* — my dearest — only *he* is a real man.

"'But I got burnt and thrown back on the ground. Something was preventing my ray from getting through to Vladimir. Once again I quickly aimed my ray at the room where he was sitting watching the video, and you know what I saw? There in front of him was this invisible energy mass — my foremother was kneeling right in front of him. Vladimir could not see or hear her. He just kept watching the tape. In the meantime my foremother was warming the wounds on Vladimir's legs with her breath, as he was pouring this terribly painful cologne on his wounds. And my foremother tried speaking to him, but he was unable to hear.

"'My foremother is so strong in spirit that nothing invisible could penetrate her. Any psychotropic weapons trained on her will explode. She will hardly pay them any attention. In any case any attack will be repelled. And there was no way I could interfere. I could only watch...

"'I watched and began thinking ever so quickly. What had happened? How did a situation like this come about? Why was the speaker saying such things? Did he want to help me? Was he trying to explain something? If so, what? Why was my ray so drawn to Vladimir? Naturally I was afraid that Vladimir might take offence at the words "not a real man" and that he would be jealous of another over me. And then suddenly... O, how painful it was! It really hurt. After Vladimir had heard the whole tape, he simply sighed and said: "Whaddya know, a real man! In Australia, I heard, eh? They are going to meet. Maybe then they will give me my son."

"'My ray began trembling. It was as though everything had somehow gone dark. You see? Vladimir was not jealous. Naturally that is not a good feeling — jealousy. But I wanted to see him jealous, at least a little. Just a teeny-weeny bit. But here was Vladimir handing me over to another with complete indifference.

"'I could not restrain myself and started to cry. I began asking, pleading with my foremother to tell me what I had done wrong. What mistake had I made? Where had I transgressed? She did not reply until Vladimir had finished binding the last wound. Then she told me sadly:

""'All you had to do was love, daughter dear. To think about what was good for your beloved without elevating yourself in the process."

"'I tried to explain that I did really want only what was good. But once again she quietly said:

""'You wanted something for *yourself*, daughter dear — pictures, music, poems and songs! It will all come to pass — your dream is powerful. I know. It is for everyone and for the one you love, too, but now it will be more and more difficult for you to obtain *earthly* love. You are becoming a star, daughter dear. People may admire and love a star as a star, but not as a woman."

"'That was the last thing my foremother said. I lost my sense of self-control, I screamed and tried to explain, to argue that I did not want to be a star, that I simply wanted to be a woman and to be loved! But nobody could hear me.

"'Please help me! There is a lot I now understand. I am not afraid for myself — I can take care of myself. But it will take Vladimir much longer to understand... And in the meantime listening to that kind of talk is leading him away from Truth.

"'The distribution of that cassette must be stopped. It suggests to people, including Vladimir, that I am some sort of ideal role model, a star, and that someone else instead of him ought to be with me.

"'I am not a star. I am a woman. I want to love whom I myself want to love.

"'My path is not determined by me alone.

"'I was mistaken. I dreamt things would work out so that people would talk about me, dedicate verses and songs to me, that artists would draw me... And that has all come about.

"'Whenever I dream, my dreams all come true. And this one has, too. I am grateful for the verses and songs. I am grateful to the poets. But I was mistaken all along. That was how I dreamt it. The poems are needed! But I was not supposed to become a star.

"'I wanted all that so Vladimir would look at the images, listen to the songs, and remember. So he would remember me. But I did not know this when I was dreaming it. Now I realise — I am becoming a star. Everyone looks up to stars. But it is a *woman* they love.'

"Anastasia, do you realise what you're asking for? There's no way to stop a cassette from being distributed, especially when it's one people copy themselves. That's not something you can control. Nobody can.'

"'You see? *You* cannot. But *Vladimir*... He is an entrepreneur. And even if it is said to be uncontrollable, *he* could still do something. But he does not want to do anything. He is resigned to the assumption that I am not a suitable mate for him.'"

Chapter Six

Forces of Light

"Boris Moiseevich," Alexander continued, "forgot about everything else and went on plying Anastasia with questions, such as:

"'What are the forces of Light?'

"'These,' Anastasia replied, 'are all the bright thoughts ever produced by people. All space is filled with them.'

"'Can you freely communicate with them? Can you see them?'

"'Yes, I can.'

"'Can you answer any question confronting science today?'

"'Many of them, perhaps. But every scientist — indeed, every Man — can find the answers. Everything depends upon the purity of one's thoughts, and the motive for asking.'

"'Could you explain certain phenomena for science?'

"'If the answer does not come to you, it means your thoughts are not sufficiently pure. Such is the law of the Creator. I will not go against it, if I feel it is not right to tell you.'

"'Is there something higher than the bright thoughts produced by Man?'

"'There is. But they are just as significant.'

"'What is it? How could you define it?'

"'In a way you are capable of relating to.'

"'Are you able to talk with Him?'

"'Yes. At least sometimes. As far as I know, I talk directly with Him.'

"'Is there some kind of energy that exists in the Universe that we don't know about on the Earth?'

"'The greatest energy in the Universe is on the Earth. We need only to understand it.'

"'Can you, Anastasia, give me at least an approximate description of this energy? Is it like a nuclear reaction? A vacuum phenomenon?'

"'The most powerful energy in the Universe is the energy of Pure Love.'

"'I'm talking about visible, tangible energy, capable of influencing technical progress, of producing heat and light. And, if you like, an explosion.'

"'And I am talking about the same thing. All your humanly established installations, taken together, are not able to supply light to the Earth for any length of time. But the energy of Love *can*.'

"'There you go talking allegorically again. In some other, metaphorical sense.'

"'I am talking in a literal sense, as *you* understand it.'

"'But love is a feeling! It's not something visible — it can't be applied, or even seen.'

"'Love is energy. It is reflected. It *is* possible to see it.'

"'Where is it reflected? How is it possible to see it?'

"'The Sun, the stars, the visible planets — they are all but reflectors of this energy. The light of the Sun, which gives life to everything on the Earth, is created by human love. In the whole Universe the energy of Love is reproduced only in the soul of Man. It takes upward flight, becomes filtered and reflected, and pours itself forth from the planets of the Universe as beneficial light upon the Earth.'

"'Do not combustive, chemical reactions take place on the Sun all on their own?'

"'You only have to do a little reasoning to realise the falsity of such a conclusion. It is like, as you put it, "two-plus-two".'

"'Can Man control this energy?'

"'Not to any significant degree, at least for the time being.'

"'But do you know how to do it?'

"'Myself, I do not know. If I knew, my beloved would already love me.'

"'You say you can communicate with *Him* — a Being higher than the forces of Light? Does He always answer you? I mean, willingly?'

"'Always. And He always answers very gently. Because He could not do otherwise.'

"'Could you ask Him how to control the energy of Love?'

"'I did ask.'

"'And?'

"'To comprehend certain answers of His, one needs to have a certain level of conscious awareness and purity, which I myself do not have. I do not understand all His answers.'

"'But you will still attempt to do something to obtain this requited love?'

"'Of course I shall do something.'

"'What will you do?'

"'I shall think. Help me. I need to ask all the women out there who have ever loved, all who have or have not been loved. They will think, analyse and produce thoughts which will appear in the dimension of the forces of Light. I shall see them. I shall understand and then I shall help everyone. Thoughts in the dimension of Light are always comprehensible.'

"'Anastasia, we can't put a question to all the women of the world at once. Nobody can do that.'

"'Then ask Vladimir. He will figure out how to do it, he will find a way. But he will not do it just for me. You will have to persuade him that this is very important for all people, for him. If he feels how important it is, he will definitely do something. He will find a way of asking all the women at once.'

"'You believe so strongly in him. Why then has he not been able to love you in return?'

"'He is not to blame. I am to blame. I made many mistakes. Possibly I was in a hurry and made myself appear too fantastic to him with my abilities. Possibly he is not yet able to appreciate why his son has to be raised in surroundings that seem unusual for human beings — that is, in the forest. Possibly I should not have interfered so drastically with his customary habits, not have intruded on his conscious awareness. I know now that men really do not like that. They can even beat women for that. I should probably have waited and he would have come to understand it all on his own. He should have felt that he is superior to me at least in something.

"'But I did not realise this in time. I told him that he could not see his son until he purified himself. At that moment I was thinking only of our son, about what was best for him, and I inadvertently said it would not be good for him to see his father as a dimwit. So it turned out that *I* was the altogether clever one, and my beloved was stupid. What kind of requited love could I dream about after that?'

"'Why then do you need to ask other women, if you are so capable of analysing things yourself?'

"'I need to determine whether there really is a possibility of setting everything right. I cannot determine this by myself, I am so emotionally wrought whenever I think about him. The analysis needs to be carried out calmly, through reminiscence and comparison. But I have nothing to reminisce about except him.'

"'And can you talk with him?'

"'I feel mere words are useless. Real love does not come out of words. Some kind of actions are required. But which ones? Perhaps one of the women will have the experience and the needed answer?'

"'And you are unable to reach him with your ray?'

"'I cannot even touch him now with my ray. My foremother's spirit is often right beside him. And she will not permit it. I know why.'"

CHAPTER SEVEN

Assault!

"The helicopter was coming in for a landing," Alexander went on. "We all watched it land without saying a word. The two crewmen got out, came over to where we were standing and fixed their eyes too on Anastasia. A group of armed, robust fellows silently stood watching this lone figure in an old cardigan standing before them, and immediately it was clear to all: they must capture this woman. The only question was: what was the most accommodating way to make the capture? After a long pause Boris Moiseevich laid it down in black and white:

"'Anastasia, you realise you represent a valuable resource for science. The decision has already been made to transfer you to the nature preserve near Moscow. This is necessary for your own good, among other things. If for some reason you don't understand the situation and refuse to come voluntarily, we shall be obliged to effect the transfer by force.

"'Naturally you will want to have your child with you in your new place. You show us the location of your glade on the map and the helicopter will go fetch your son. Later we can capture a few of the animals and transport them to your new dwelling-place. I repeat: all this is necessary for your own benefit, for the benefit of your son and other people as well. You *do* want to bring benefit to people, don't you?'

"'Yes,' Anastasia replied calmly, and right away added: 'Everything I know I am ready to share with all people, if they find it interesting, but only with *all* people. Science is not something that is available to everybody at once. Its achievements are used first only by localised groups, often for their selfish, personal interests. The vast majority get to know about only what the localised groups are disposed to reveal.

"'Who do you represent? Is it not a particular localised group? I cannot go with you. I need to raise a Man, I need to raise my son. That can only be done properly where a Space of Love has been created. This Space has been created and perfected by my forebears, near and distant. It is still small, but it is what ties me to the whole substance of the Universe. Every Man must create around himself his own Space of Love, and offer it to his child. Bearing children without preparing a Space of Love for them is criminal. Every Man must create around himself a small Space of Love. And if everyone understood this and acted upon it, then the whole Earth would become the brightest focus of Love in the Universe. This is the way He wanted it, and this is Man's purpose. For only Man is capable of creating such a Space.'

"Two strong security men approached Anastasia from behind, one on either side. It wasn't clear whether they were acting on orders from the security captain or whether it had all been planned out in advance. They exchanged glances and simultaneously grabbed Anastasia's arms. They did this quite professionally, though not without a certain degree of apprehension. They kept a tight grip on her arms, as though holding a captured bird by its outspread wings.

"The security captain was a stocky fellow, his hair cut real short. He stepped out in front and stood beside Boris Moiseevich. Anastasia's face showed no sign of fear. But she was no longer looking at us. Her head was slightly inclined toward the ground, her eyelids were lowered, hiding her gaze. And she began to speak without raising her eyes, with the same calm and gentleness in her voice as before.

"'Please do not use force. It is dangerous.'

"'For whom?' the security captain enquired in a raspy voice.

"'For you. And it would be unpleasant for me.'

"Boris Moiseevich tried to restrain what may have been either his fear or his excitement. He asked Anastasia:

"'Can you cause us physical pain using supernatural abilities?'

"'I am Man. A Man, like anybody else. But I am worried. Worry may allow undesirable things to happen.'

"'Such as?'

"'Matter... cells... atoms... nuclei... nuclear particles in chaotic movement... You know about them. If one visualises them vividly and in full detail, perceives and understands them properly, and then uses the full powers of one's imagination to extract from the nucleus even a single chaotically moving particle, then the matter begins... begins to...'

"Anastasia turned her head to one side, lifted her eyelids just slightly and fixed her gaze on a stone lying on the ground. The stone immediately began to break apart into small particles and before long was transformed into a pile of sand. Then she raised her gaze to the security captain, squinting her eyes into a concentrated stare. Steam began to escape from the tip of the security captain's left ear. The tendon slowly, millimetre by millimetre, began to disappear, and suddenly the young guard standing beside him went white with fear and drew his pistol from its holster. He did it automatically, like a professional soldier, without thinking. He aimed the pistol directly at Anastasia and discharged the whole cartridge.

"No doubt the thoughts of each one of us at that moment were racing at top speed, and something happened which you occasionally hear about with soldiers in wartime, when in extreme conditions they see a grenade or a bullet in motion. And even though the grenade or bullet is flying at its usual speed, the acceleration of one's thinking and perceptive faculties causes it to be seen as in slow motion.

"I watched as the bullets from the frightened security guard's gun flew at Anastasia one after another. The first bullet grazed her temple. The rest of the bullets never reached her — they dissolved into dust while still in flight, just like the stone which she had trained her gaze upon earlier.

"We all stood there stupefied. We stood and watched as a stream of blood flowed down Anastasia's cheek from under her kerchief.

"The guards holding Anastasia by the arms stepped back from her when they heard the gunshots, but didn't let go of her. They had got her in a death-grip, and were pulling her in opposite directions.

"All at once a pale-bluish glow flooded the ground around us. It came from somewhere up above and quickly intensified. It dazzled us, making us incapable of moving or speaking. In the unusual quiet that followed we heard Anastasia say:

"'Please, let go my arms. I may not be able to... Let go, please.'

"But the petrified guards did not let go their death-grip. Now I realise why she raised her arm in a characteristic gesture when she was talking with you. It was this gesture that indicated to someone up above that everything was in order and that she did not need help. But this time they wouldn't let her raise her arm.

"The bluish glow continued to intensify, then something seemed to sparkle, and we saw — we saw a fiery sphere hanging over us, pulsating with a pale-blue light. It was like a huge ball lightning. And inside it were sparkling networks of hundreds of lightning discharges. Occasionally they would spark out beyond the blue membrane-like hull and reach the tops of the nearby trees, or even the flowers beneath our feet, but caused them no harm. One of the thin lightning bolts momentarily made contact with an obstruction which rocks and a fallen tree had made in the creek; it transformed the obstruction into a cloud of dust which instantly vaporised.

"The bolts that sparked out beyond the blue hull of the fiery sphere no doubt possessed tremendous power of an energy we know nothing about. It seemed as though it was being controlled by some kind of intelligence.

"We had the impression of being in the presence of an intelligent being which possessed unimaginable power. But the most incredible and unnatural thing about what was taking place were the sensations we felt from its presence. We had no sense of fear or suspicion — on the contrary...

"You can just imagine — right there in a situation like that we began to feel a sense of calm and grace, as though something very close to us, something related to us, had suddenly appeared.

"At that point the pulsating blue sphere soared over our heads and seemed to be studying us, sizing up the situation. All at once it made a circle in the air and landed at Anastasia's feet. The bluish glow intensified and, like a pleasing languor, relaxed us to the point where we simply didn't feel like moving, or even hearing or saying anything.

"The blue hull of the sphere then emitted several fiery bolts at once. They swept over to Anastasia, began touching her, as though stroking the toes of her bare feet.

"Anastasia managed to free her arms from the languishing security guards. She stretched out her arms toward the sphere. Immediately it rose to the level of her face, and the lightning bolts, which we had seen with our eyes turn to dust the stones piled up in the creek, began to fondle her arms, while doing them no harm.

"Anastasia began talking with the sphere. We couldn't distinguish any words but, judging by her gestures and facial expression, she was trying to explain something to it, to prove or persuade it of the way she was seeing something, but without success. The sphere gave no response to her, but it was nevertheless clear that it was not agreeing with her. This much was evident, since Anastasia went on trying to persuade it with considerable excitement. It was the excitement that no doubt caused her cheeks to flush. Still talking away, she removed her kerchief. Golden wheat-coloured braids of hair hung about Anastasia's shoulders and covered the stream of dried blood on her face. We saw how perfectly beautiful her facial features were.

"The fiery sphere made several revolutions, like a comet, around Anastasia's head, then stopped once more in front of her face, and a thousand delicate lightning bolts swept through her golden hair, neatly touching each individual strand, lifting and stroking them. One of the bolts lifted a whole bunch of strands at once and opened the bullet wound in her temple, while another bolt began gliding along the traces of the dried blood. It was as though the sphere was using the actions of its lightning bolts in place of words to remind Anastasia about what had happened and to contradict her arguments.

"Finally all the little bolts drew back inside the sphere. Anastasia lowered her head and fell silent. The sphere made one more revolution around her and then rose into the air. The bluish glow decreased in intensity, and we felt things gradually return toward the way they were before, but instead of the bluish light a brown smoke now began rising from the earth. This smoke filled the whole space around us, and only Anastasia remained in a little circle of blue. And when this brownish smoke completely enveloped us, that was when we began to discover what hell really is."

Chapter Eight

What hell is

"Old Bible pictures showing the beastly torture of sinners over hot coals, and even the most extreme portrayals of horror-film monsters, pale like children's innocent fairy-tales in comparison to the hell we went through there on the riverbank!" Alexander exclaimed. "Since the beginning of time mankind has never managed to dream up anything that can compare with it. All the Bible images and horror films stop at depicting all the different ways fleshly bodies can be torn apart and dismembered, which is nothing by comparison with real hell."

"But what could be more frightful than the acute torturing of the flesh?" I queried. "What kind of hell did you see?"

"Once the blue glow had weakened sufficiently to allow the brownish smoke to rise from the earth and it had enveloped us completely from head to toe, we found ourselves split into two halves."

"What two halves?"

"Just imagine — I suddenly found myself comprised of two component parts. The first was my body, enveloped in a transparent skin through which I could see all my internal organs — my heart, stomach, intestines, the blood rushing through my veins, along with various other organs. The other part — invisible — consisted of my feelings, my emotions, my mind, my desires, my pain sensibility — in other words, everything about Man that you can't see."

"What's the difference whether the parts are together or separated, as long as it's still you? What happened to you that was so awful, aside from seeing your skin transparent?"

"The difference turned out to be incredibly significant. The thing is, our bodies began to act on their own, independently of our minds, wills, aspirations or desires. We could observe the actions of our bodies from an external viewpoint, yet our feelings and pain sensibilities remained with our invisible selves, and we were deprived of any ability to influence the actions of our own bodies."

"Like someone who's terribly drunk?"

"Drunks don't see themselves externally, at least not while they're drunk, whereas we saw and felt everything. Our clarity of consciousness was extraordinarily acute. I could see how beautiful the grass, the flowers and the river looked. I could hear the birds singing and the creek burbling away, I could feel the cleanness of the air around me, along with the warmth of the sunbeams. But those bodies... All the transparent bodies standing in our group suddenly trotted down, like a herd of sheep, to a pond formed by the creek.

"The pond resembled a little lake, the water in it was clear and transparent, the bottom was covered with soft sand and beautiful stones. Tiny fish were swimming in it. Our bodies ran down to this splendid little lake and started splashing around in it. They started urinating and defecating in it.

"The water became dirty and clouded, yet our bodies began drinking from it. I saw the dirty, stinking liquid flow through my intestines and into my stomach. I was overcome with a sensation of nausea and revulsion.

"Then under one of the trees by the pond all at once appeared the naked bodies of two women. Their skin was just as transparent as that of our bodies.

"The women's bodies lay down on the grass under the tree, lolling about and stretching out in the warm sunshine. My body and that of the security captain ran over to the women's bodies.

"My body began stroking one of the women's bodies, it felt a responding caress and entered into sexual intercourse with the woman's body. The security captain's approach was not reciprocated and his body started raping the woman. Then one of the guards came running over and started hitting first my spine and then my head with a rock, but it was I, and not my body, that felt excruciating pain. The guard dragged my body away from the woman's and started raping her himself.

"Our bodies soon began to grow old and decrepit. It was as though time was accelerating everything. The woman that had just been raped now became pregnant, and through her transparent skin you could see the embryo taking form and enlarging itself in the womb.

"The body of the scientist, Boris Moiseevich, went over to the pregnant woman, and spent some time peering attentively through her transparent skin at the developing embryo. Then all of a sudden he slipped his hand into the woman's vagina, and began wrenching out the fœtus.

"In the meantime, Stanislav's body was quickly collecting rocks into a pile, then wildly breaking off small trees and using them, along with any other materials he found handy, to construct something resembling a cabin. My body went over to help. When the cabin was just about finished, my body tried to kick Stanislav's body out of the cabin; he resisted and our bodies started fighting with each other.

"Even though I myself was invisible, I could still feel terrible pain when he started hitting the legs and head of my body. Our fight caught the attention of the other bodies, and they shoved us both out of the cabin, and then started fighting for it amongst themselves. My body became terribly frail and began decomposing before my very eyes. It could no longer walk, and just lay there under a bush, wasting away with a nauseating stench. Worms appeared on my body, and I could feel them crawling all over me, creeping into my internal organs and eating away at them. I acutely felt them gnawing away at my insides, and awaited the final decomposition of my body to escape from this excruciating torture.

"Then all at once a fœtus emerged from the second woman that had been raped. It began to grow right before my eyes. Soon the little fellow stood up and took its first timid step, then another, then it staggered and fell on its bottom. I could feel a painful sensation as it landed, and I realised to my horror that this was my new body and it was doomed to survive — to exist among these abominable, brainless bodies, which were desecrating themselves and everything around.

"I realised that I, who was invisible, would never die and that I was condemned to eternal contemplation and an acute awareness of the nastiness of everything that was going on, experiencing physical and even more terrible pain.

"The same thing was happening with the other bodies. They decayed, decomposed and were born again, and with each new birth our bodies simply switched roles.

"There was hardly any vegetation left around. In its place ugly structures had appeared, and the once pristine pond had been transformed into a stinking cesspool."

Alexander fell silent. I too felt a sense of revulsion from what he had said, but not pity.

"Indeed," I said, "you all went through a horrible experience, but you vermin had it coming to you. How come you had to latch on to Anastasia? She lives all alone in the taiga, she doesn't touch anybody, doesn't ask for housing, she doesn't require a pension or any kind of amenities, so why go interfering with her?"

Alexander didn't give any sign of offence to my verbal attack on him. He simply sighed and responded:

"You know, you said we 'went through an experience'. But, you see... It may seem hard to believe, but the thing is, I'm not completely out of it. I think those who were in our group, too, haven't fully come out of it."

"What do you mean, 'haven't fully'? Here you are, sitting calmly beside me, poking the ashes in the fire..."

"Yeah, sure I'm sitting here poking the ashes, but that acute awareness of something terrible has stayed with me. It still frightens me. This terrible thing is not just in the past — it is still going with us today, right now. With all of us."

"Maybe something's happening with *you,* but everything's okay with me and everyone else."

"But doesn't it seem to you, Vladimir, that the situation we were in is an exact copy of what mankind is doing today? What we were shown in a microcosm and at an accelerated speed only reflects what's going on today in the world."

"It doesn't seem that way to me, since our skin is not transparent and our bodies obey our commands."

"Maybe someone's just taking pity on us, not letting us become fully aware of what we have done and are continuing to do. After all, if we were aware of it, if we could see our lives from an external viewpoint, we'd see them exposed, along with all the false teachings which we've used through the ages to justify what we are doing. We wouldn't last, we'd go out of our minds!

"We try to put on a decent front, we try to justify the evil we do by our own so-called 'insurmountable weaknesses'. We couldn't resist temptation: we started smoking and drinking, committed murder, then we started going to war to defend some sort of ideals. We started setting off bombs.

"We are weak. That's the way we see ourselves today. We say there are higher powers — they can do everything, they decide everything. But as for us? We hide behind dogmas like that and feel we can get away with any kind of filth we like.

"And let's face it, what we do *is* filth. We all do it, every one of us, only we justify it to ourselves in different ways. But now it is absolutely clear that, as long as my consciousness has not lost its control over my body, I and I alone must take personal responsibility for all its actions. And Anastasia is right when she says 'As long as Man is in the flesh...'"

"Don't go citing Anastasia, smart ass! 'She is right!' But you yourself practically had her in the grave. Too bad she didn't go just a little further and then you would all have lost your marbles completely!"

I was really growing more and more angry at the whole bunch of them, but since Alexander was the only one in front of me, he had to bear the brunt of my anger.

"Just look at your own self," Alexander replied. "Wasn't it thanks to you that we were able to get through to Anastasia? And not just us — you think attempts like ours won't be repeated?

"Whatever possessed you to specify the exact name of your ship, even the name of your captain? Don't play the documentarian. You could even have changed the name of the river, but you didn't do it — you didn't think of it in time. And here you expect others to always know the right thing to do. I got what was coming to me. Now my whole life I will have to keep making sense of that nightmare I witnessed."

"Tell me, how did it end, that nightmare of yours? How did you get out of it?"

"We would never have been able to come out of it all on our own. It was something we were to go on reliving forever. At least that was the impression each of us had.

"Anastasia appeared amidst our decomposing and still active bodies. *Her* skin wasn't transparent. She was still wearing her old cardigan and long skirt. She tried speaking to our bodies, but they wouldn't listen. They seemed to be preprogrammed to die and be born again, repeating their actions over and over with only a change of roles.

"At that point Anastasia started quickly picking up the garbage near one of the structures our bodies had built. She quickly gathered the scattered stones and brush into a pile with her hands, loosened the earth a little with a stick, touched and fluffed up the grass where we had trampled it, and the little green blades began popping up again — not all, but those that still could. Anastasia carefully straightened the broken trunk of a small tree, about a metre tall: she mashed up some earth in her hands to soften it and then daubed it on the broken part of the tree. She squeezed the tree between her hands, and held it tight for a while. Then, when she carefully took her hands away, the tree remained upright.

"Anastasia nimbly went on doing what she had to do. She created a small 'oasis' on the ground our bodies had trampled, which had been left almost devoid of vegetation. Boris Moiseevich's body ran over to it, leapt onto the grass and rolled around on it, then jumped up and ran off. A little while later it returned with the body of one of the guards. Together they uprooted the small tree and began dragging stones and sticks to the 'oasis', where they attempted to put together yet another ugly-looking plain structure.

"Anastasia threw up her hands in frustration. She tried talking to them but, as she met no response, she apparently abandoned her efforts at persuasion. After standing for a while in a dither about what to do next, she dropped to her knees, covered her face with her hands, and you could see the hair trembling on her shoulders. Anastasia was crying — crying just like a baby.

"And almost immediately the bluish glow reappeared, at first barely noticeable. It drove the brownish smoke of our hell into the ground and reunited our bodies and our minds. Only we still weren't able to move about — but this time it wasn't from horror, but from a sweet and pleasant languor emanating from the blue glow. The fiery sphere was again circling overhead.

"Anastasia stretched out her hands toward it. The sphere instantly changed location to within a metre of her face. She began talking with it, and this time I could distinguish words. Anastasia told the sphere:

"'Thank you. You are kind. Thank you for your mercy and your love. The people will understand, they will most certainly understand everything, they will understand it in their hearts. Do not ever take your beautiful blue light from the Earth, your light of love.'

"Anastasia smiled, and a tiny tear rolled down her cheek. From the sphere's pale-blue membrane hull fiery lightning bolts flew into her face. Carefully and dexterously they picked up the tear on her cheek, glistening in the sun, and ever so delicately, as though it were a priceless gem, held the tear on their fiery tips as they placed it inside the sphere. The sphere gave a shudder, executed a circle around Anastasia, landed momentarily at her feet, then swept upward and dissolved into the blue sky above, leaving everything on the ground the way it was before.

"And there we were, standing where we had been before. The sun was shining, the river was flowing as it had always done, the forest could be seen rising in the distance, and there was Anastasia standing in front of us, right where she had been earlier. We stood there silently taking in everything around us. I was overjoyed by what I saw, and I think the others were, too. Only we weren't talking — perhaps because of what we had experienced and the natural surroundings which had suddenly become so beautiful to our gaze."

Alexander fell silent, as though he had quite withdrawn into himself. I tried speaking to him:

"Listen, Alexander, maybe everything you told me really didn't happen that way at all. Maybe Anastasia's simply able to use some sort of powerful hypnosis? I've read that there are many recluses who can do that. So maybe she hypnotised you and showed you a vision?"

"Hypnosis, you say? Did you notice the grey streaks in my hair?"

"Yes, I did."

"Those grey streaks appeared after this all happened."

"But you could have got a huge fright under hypnosis, and that caused the grey streaks."

"Well, if you assume it was hypnosis, then there's another mystery you'll have to explain."

"And what's that?"

"The stone and log obstruction in the creek. It's completely disappeared — the creek runs freely now. But the obstruction was there before our 'vision' — everybody saw it — it was there!"

"Okay... That's something to think about."

"Anyway, what difference does it make what happened to us. There's something more important than that. I'm not the same person I was before — I don't know how to live now, what I should be studying, or where. After I got home, I burnt a lot of my books written by different so-called sages, 'wise men', teachers from various parts of the world. I had quite a decent-sized personal library."

"What d'you go and do that for? You should have sold them, if you no longer needed them."

"I couldn't sell them. I didn't even think of selling them. Now I have some accounts to settle with those teachers and sages."

"And what do you think, Alexander — is it dangerous to communicate with Anastasia? Maybe she really is some kind of anomaly? After all some of the letters I've got say that she represents another civilisation. If that's true, then it'd be dangerous to communicate with her, because you never know what this other civilisation might have in mind."

"I think just the opposite is true," Alexander replied. "She has such a feeling and love for the Earth, for everything living and growing on it, that, compared to Anastasia, we look pretty much like vagrant aliens."

"Then *who is she?* Can scientists say for sure, once and for all? How did she manage to acquire such a huge mass of information? Where does she have room to store it in her head? Where did she get her mystifying abilities? What about her ray?"

"I think we simply have to go by her words here — she said: 'I am Man, I am a woman'. As for all that information, I don't think she stores any of it in her head. I think, rather, that the purity of her thoughts allows her access to the database of the entire Universe. And that her talents derive from this total access to information.

"The Universe loves *her,* but is wary of *us,* and that's why it won't open itself to us completely. Our thoughts — the thoughts of any Man raised in today's society — are blocked by stereotypes and conventions, in contrast to her thought, which is completely open and free. That's why it's hard for us to explain her mysterious abilities simply by her assertion that she is Man.

"Of course she can perform incredible feats — miracles, in our perception — I know that from personal experience. During our visit one other incident happened which can *only* be described as a miracle. It's even more mystifying than what happened with our group. And much grander!"

Alexander uttered these last few words with a certain degree of excitement in his voice. He got up and walked away from the fire into the night. In the twinkling light of the stars and the dusky glow from the smouldering fire I could see the young Siberian lad pacing back and forth. I could hear his brief, excited phrases. Alexander was saying something incomprehensible about science, and psychologists, and some sort of teachings. I got tired of sitting there and listening to his fragmentary utterances. I was dying to hear what kind of 'grand miracle' he had seen Anastasia perform.

I tried to calm him down.

"Relax, Alexander, sit down. Tell me more specifically, what grand thing you witnessed?"

Alexander tossed some dry branches onto the fire and sat down again beside it. But I could see he had not fully regained his composure. Out of nervousness, no doubt, he had stirred the smouldering coals so forcefully that the sparks flying upward landed on him and on me, causing us to jump up and away from the fire. When things had quieted down, I began listening to his emotional tale.

"In the space of some twenty minutes," he began, "Anastasia managed to change right before our eyes the physical condition of a little village girl. She did this before our very eyes. And over this period of time she changed not only the little girl's destiny, but her mother's too, and even had an effect on the whole outward appearance of this remote Siberian village. And it all happened within the space of twenty minutes or so. The main thing was *how* she did it — simplicity itself! She...

"How can anyone believe in horoscopes after that?!" Alexander wondered. "I saw it happen! That's why I burnt my books with all that 'wise man' nonsense and all that religious stuff."

"See," I countered, "you yourself admit that she performs superhuman miracles, mystical wonders, even if she smashes horoscopes in the process. She makes these things happen all by herself, and then expects to be called a normal human being. If only she'd tried to *act* half-way normal, but no!... I spoke to her about that, too — I said she should just act like everyone else, then everything will be normal, but it seems she's not capable of acting like everyone else. Pity! She's such a kind and beautiful woman, so smart — she can heal people, and she's borne me a son... But to live with her, the way I'd live with another woman — well, that's simply impossible. I can't imagine anybody being able to sleep with her after everything you've told me. Nobody could. Everybody needs a *woman,* plain and simple, not a far-out eccentric like that. But she herself is to blame for that, what with her mysticism and all."

"Hold on, Vladimir. Now it's my turn to tell *you* something. Just think carefully about what I'm going to say. It may seem incredible, but try to understand. Everybody has to understand it! *Everybody!* Perhaps, together, we can make some sense out of it. Perhaps...

"You see, Vladimir, Anastasia performed this incredible miracle with the little girl, but there was no mystery or magic involved. No sorcery, no shamanistic gimmicks. If you can imagine, she, Anastasia, did this miracle using just simple human words known to everyone. Simple, everyday words, only spoken in the right place at the right time.

"If psychologists were to analyse Anastasia's conversation with this little village girl, they would realise how psychologically effective it is. Anyone uttering these same words could have achieved a similar effect. But to have these words come to mind at the right time, the sincerity and purity of thought Anastasia spoke of are an absolute requirement."

"So, it's not just good enough to memorise the words?"

"We've all known them for a long time — that's not the point. The real question is: what lies *behind* each of the words we say?"

"Somehow you're losing me. You'd better tell me the rest of what happened with you there. What words could change people's physical condition and their whole destinies?"

"All right. Of course I should explain. Listen."

CHAPTER NINE

When words change destinies

"After what we experienced," Alexander began, "our group took a while to regain a sense of normalcy. Nobody spoke with anyone else. We stood there right in the same spot and it was only after some time had passed that we began to look to either side of us and take in the surrounding world in a different way from before, as though we were sensing it for the first time. And now we noticed a group of residents approaching us from the direction of the village. The local population was quite small, only about a dozen people lived in the six houses of this remote Siberian settlement. And they were nearly all oldsters, some of them quite frail. One woman was bent over double — she walked with a limp, carried a cane, but she still came with the others. Those who did not require a walking stick were armed with various tools — one carried a cross-beam, another an oar. They had evidently come to defend Anastasia. These old and frail people were advancing against young, healthy, stalwart fellows carrying weapons. They advanced without fear, determined to come to Anastasia's defence, no matter who might be standing in their way.

"Their resolve was terrifying. When they drew near to us, the old fellow carrying the oar and wearing rubber boots, who was walking slightly ahead of the others, stopped, which brought a halt to the group of villagers as a whole. They paid no attention to us, treating our group as empty space. With a sedate stroke of his beard he looked right at Anastasia and greeted her respectfully:

"'I wish you good health, my dear, dear Anastasia, on behalf of all of us.'

"'Good day to you, kind people,' Anastasia responded, clasping her hand to her breast and bowing to the elderly villagers.

"'The water in the river is dropping early this year,' the old fellow went on. 'The summer hasn't been too rainy.'

"'Not so rainy just now,' Anastasia confirmed, 'but more rain will come, the water level will rise, and the river will return to its former strength.'

"As they continued talking that way, out from the group of elderly villagers emerged a frail little girl, about six years old, with pale yellowish skin. She was wearing an old jacket, pieced together from fragments of some adult garment, her thin legs were covered by patched pantyhose, and she had little old boots on her feet.

"Later I found out the girl's name was Aniuta. She was a sickly child, with a congenital heart disease. Her mother had brought her from the city when she was just six months old and left her with the oldsters, not coming back even once to see her daughter. They say she works somewhere as a painter for a construction firm.

"Aniuta went up to Anastasia and started tugging on the hem of her skirt, pleading with her:

"'Bend down, Auntie Anastasia. Bend down to me.'

"Anastasia looked at the little girl and squatted down in front of her. The girl quickly took off the old white kerchief she was wearing on her head. She salivated on one edge of it and began to carefully wipe the blood which had already dried on Anastasia's face and temple, saying:

"'You don't come any more, Auntie Anastasia, to sit on your little log by the shore. Grandpa said that earlier you used to come more often. You would sit on the log and watch the river. Now you don't come. Grandpa showed me the little log where you used to sit, Auntie Anastasia. Grandpa showed me, and I started coming to it, to your log, myself. I sat there all alone, waiting for you to come, Auntie Anastasia. I really wanted to see you. I have a secret to tell you. But you wouldn't come to sit on your log and watch the river. Maybe 'cause the log is quite old. I kept asking Grandpa and he brought a new little log for you. There it is, lying right beside the old one.'

"The little girl took Anastasia by the hand and started pulling her over to the log.

"'Let's go, let's go, Auntie Anastasia, let's go sit on the new log. Grandpa hewed out two seats on it with his axe. I was the one who asked him to do that, so that when you came we could sit together.'

"Anastasia at once responded to the little girl's request, and they sat down together on the log. They just sat there silently for a while, not paying any attention to anyone. It was as though there had been no one else around. And everyone stood silently, without budging. Then the little girl started talking:

"'Grandma told me a lot about you, Auntie Anastasia. And when my Grandma died, I began asking Grandpa, and he told me about you, too. Whenever Grandpa talks about you, I think about my little secret I have to tell you. Grandpa told me that when I was little, my heart wasn't working right. It wasn't ticking evenly. One time its tick was way off. Then they brought in Auntie Doctor in a boat. Auntie Doctor said there was nothing they could do with such a bad heart — there was no one it would obey. And that it would die before long.

"'Grandpa told me how you, Auntie Anastasia, were sitting at the time on your old little log and watching the river. Then you got up and came into our hut. You took me in your arms and put me on the grass outside the house. Then you lay down beside me and put your hand on my chest. You put your hand here, where you could hear my heart ticking. Right here.' And the girl clasped her hand to the left side of her thin little chest.

"'Grandpa said that you too, Auntie Anastasia, started lying next to me as if you were breathless, since your own heart had started ticking ever so softly, just like mine. Then your heart started beating faster, and called out to mine to catch up. My heart obeyed yours, and together they started ticking the way they ought to. That is what Grandpa told me. Did he tell me everything right? Right, Auntie Anastasia?'

"'Yes, Aniuta. Your grandpa told you right. Your heart will always be good now.'

"'That means your heart called to mine and mine obeyed? It obeyed, did it?'

"'Yes, Aniuta dear, your heart obeyed.'

"'Now I shall tell you my secret, Auntie Anastasia. It is a very, very important secret!'

"'Tell me your important secret, Aniuta.'

"Aniuta got up from the log and stood in front of Anastasia, clasping her thin little hands to her chest. Then all of a sudden she... Suddenly little Aniuta fell on her knees before Anastasia. She barely managed to restrain the excitement in her voice when she said:

"'Auntie Anastasia, dear Auntie Anastasia, ask your heart again! Ask it! Ask your heart to call to my Mama's heart. Have my Mama come see me. Even just for a day. To see *me*. That's my secret. Have your heart... Mama's... heart... hear...'

"Aniuta choked from emotion, then fell silent, her eyes fixed on Anastasia.

"Anastasia squinted her eyes and looked off into the distance, past the little girl kneeling in front of her. Then she looked at the girl once more and quietly stated a fact that must have been horrifying for the child. She answered her as she would have an adult:

"'Aniuta, dear, my heart is unable to call to your Mama. Your Mama is far away in the city. She tried to find happiness but did not find it. She does not have a home of her own, she does not have any money to buy you gifts. And unless she can bring you gifts she does not want to come and see you. It is hard for her in the city. But if she *should* come and see you, it will be even harder for her. A visit with you would become a sad and tormenting experience. It would be more difficult and frightening for her to see you so sickly and so poorly clothed. She would see how the houses in your village are falling apart, and how dirty and shabby the house you live in is. It would be all the more difficult since your Mama no longer believes she can do anything good for you. She simply does not believe it. She feels she has tried everything and this is what fate has determined for her. She has given in to the very hopelessness she has imagined for herself.'

"Little Aniuta listened to the terrible truth, and her wee body trembled. It seemed to me awfully cruel to talk to a child that way. I thought a white lie would have been more appropriate here. Like stroking the poor little girl's head and promising her mother would arrive soon. And saying they would have a happy meeting.

"But that is not what Anastasia did. She told this helpless, defenceless little girl the whole bitter truth. Then after spending some time watching her body shake all over, she began talking to her again.

"'I know, Aniuta dear, you do love your Mama.'

"'I love... love... I love my poor dear Mamochka,' the girl replied, her child's voice on the point of breaking into tears.

"'Then you make your Mamochka happy. You are the only one, the only one in all the world who can make her happy. It is very simple. You become healthy and strong, and learn how to sing. You will be a singer. Your marvellous, pure voice will sing together with your heart. Your Mama may meet

you in twenty years, and seeing you will make her very happy.
Or your Mama may come to see you next summer. By that
time you should already be healthy and strong. To welcome
her. Get some presents ready for your Mamochka. Show
her how strong and beautiful you are, and you will make your
Mamochka very happy, and your meeting with her will be a
joyful one indeed.'

"'But I will never be able to be healthy or strong.'

"'Why not?'

"'You know Auntie Doctor? She wears a white coat. Auntie
Doctor told Grandma. I heard her say I'll always be a weak-
ling 'cause I was a bottle baby. My Mama wasn't able to give
me any mother's milk. My Mama had no milk in her breasts.
And children, when they are small, always drink milk from
their mama's breasts.

"'I saw it once, when a lady came to the village with a little
baby. I went over to the house she had come to. I really wanted
to see how babies drink milk from their mother's teats. I tried
to sit there ever so quietly. But they kept chasing me out. The
mama-lady wondered why I was sitting there without blink-
ing. I was afraid to blink my eyes in case I missed something.'

"'Do not you think, Aniuta, that Auntie Doctor might
have been mistaken when she said you would never be
healthy and strong?'

"'How could she have been mistaken? She wears a white
coat. Everybody listens to her — the grandfathers and grandmothers. She knows everything. She knows that I was a bottle baby.'

"'And why did you go to see how babies are breast-fed?'

"'I thought I would see how good the baby felt when he got
fed from his mother's teat. I thought I would see how good
he felt, and then I would feel better, too.'

"'You will get better, Aniuta dear. You will be healthy and
strong,' Anastasia said quietly and confidently. And then

Anastasia gradually unbuttoned her cardigan and exposed her breasts.

"Aniuta stared at the exposed breasts in amazement, quite overwhelmed by the unexpected action. From the ends of the nipples tiny drops of breast milk emerged.

"'Milk! Mother's milk! Auntie Anastasia, are you feeding a baby, too? Are you a mama?'

"'This milk is to feed my little son.'

"Drops of breast milk kept coming. One of the drops fluttered in a passing breeze. The breeze tore the drop from Anastasia's breast.

"Like a lightning-fast steel spring, Aniuta dashed after the little drop of breast milk. And she... Imagine, this thin, sickly little girl was nimble enough to catch the drop! She fell to the ground, but as she was falling she put out the palms of her hands and caught the little drop of breastmilk! She caught it just as it reached the ground. Getting up on her knees, she lifted her cupped hands to her face and opened them, examining the tiny wet spot they were holding. Then she held out her hands to Anastasia.

"'Here. I caught it. Here it is. Your son's milk is not lost.'

"'You saved the little drop, Aniuta. Now it belongs to you.'

"'To me?!'

"'Yes. Just to you.'

"Aniuta raised her cupped hands to her face and touched the drop with her lips. The frail little girl closed her eyes and held her hands pressed against her lips for a long time. Then she dropped her hands, looked at Anastasia, and with a voice full of gratitude, whispered:

"'Thank you.'

"'Come close to me, Aniuta dear.'

"Anastasia took hold of the little girl by her shoulders. She stroked her hair, then sat her on her lap. She gently inclined the little one's head to her breast, as she would an infant, and began singing quietly.

"Aniuta's lips were now very close to one of Anastasia's nipples. Almost in a half-sleep, Aniuta slowly drew her lips closer and closer to Anastasia's breast, felt the moist nipple, gave a tiny shudder and began greedily sucking on Anastasia's milk-filled breast.

"Judging by the tape recording, she awakened about nine minutes later. She raised her head and jumped down from Anastasia's lap.

"'I... Oh, dear, what have I done? I've drunk up your son's milk.'

"'Not to worry, Aniuta. There is enough left for him. You only drank the milk from one of my breasts, and there is still milk left in the other one. There is enough for him. My son can also eat pollen from the flowers if he wants to. And now you have been provided with all you need, so you will have no fear about being strong and beautiful and happy. Now go and draw your happiness from life, from each day it brings.'

"'I shall be strong and healthy. I shall think about how to greet Mamochka, so that she will not find it difficult to see me, but she will be extremely happy. Only I shan't be able to sing. I used to sing with Grandma. Then Grandma died. I keep asking Grandpa, but he doesn't sing. Only when he drinks vodka will he sing me a song, and then I sing along with him. But it is hard for me to sing along with him, 'cause his voice croaks. I also tried to sing along with the radio, but our old receiver crackles so much I can't get the words.'

"Aniuta dear, just try singing without words, try to imitate the birds when you hear them sing, or the water when it burbles, or the rustling of the leaves and the wind when it is strong and whistles through the branches. And there are a lot of sounds in the grass. You will hear many pure sounds around you if you are willing to listen. Try imitating them with your voice. They will be your best teachers...

"'I am going now, Aniuta, good-bye. It is time for me to go.'

"Anastasia got up from the log. Aniuta remained sitting, listening to the world of sounds around her. Anastasia went up to the young guard who had shot at her. The guard was still very pale in the face, and his hands were shaking. His pistol was lying nearby on the ground. Anastasia told the guard:

"'Do not blame yourself, do not torture your soul. It was not a partner in what you did. You acted out of instinct. You were trained to protect whatever you were ordered to, without thinking about the situation. And your instinct took its course. It is not good for instinct to gain supremacy in Man. When instinct takes first place, then Man takes second place. The result is something less than a Man. Think about it — perhaps it would be better to return to yourself — to the Man that you are.'

"When the guard heard the calming tones of Anastasia's voice his hands stopped shaking, and the paleness disappeared from his face. And by the time she had finished speaking, his face was flush with a reddish colour, right to the tips of his ears.

"Then Anastasia said good-bye to the elderly villagers and headed off in the direction of the taiga. For a long time we watched her as she drew further and further away. Then all at once we heard an extraordinarily pure child's voice singing.

"Aniuta was still sitting on the log, singing a beautiful, old-time song — probably one she had learnt from her grandmother. And how she sang! Her pure voice hit unusually high notes, filling the space around and enchanting the heart:

> *Sprinkling raindrops glisten.*
> *Brother rocks his sister,*
> *Brother rocks his sister,*
> *Sings to her — she listens.*

"Aniuta finished her song and began staring at our group, still standing there motionless. Then she got up, picked up a thin stick from the ground and said:

"'You chaps are bad. You're so big, but you're still bad.'

"After saying this she started coming at us, armed with the little stick. The group of elderly villagers shuffled silently along behind her. And all of us to a man began withdrawing before them. We retreated right back to our ship which was docked by the riverbank, then scrambled up the gangplank, not without some pushing and shoving. We were on the point of pulling up the gangplank when the captain suddenly noticed the two helicopter pilots were also on board.

"'How come you're here?' he shouted from the bridge. 'Who's looking after the chopper?'

"The pilots jumped down from the ship and ran over to their 'copter.

"We left, abandoning the barrels of fuel and tents remaining on the shore. Nobody even thought of collecting them."

CHAPTER TEN

Work out your own happiness

When Alexander finished his story, I couldn't help expressing
my animosity toward him.

"I see only too well what you're up to. So you left the tents
there. And the barrels too, eh? Too bad you got away with just
some grey hair. She's a holy person, Anastasia. It was so clear
straight off — any normal person who'd seen you would have
twigged what was going on, right off the bat. They would have
known who was standing in front of them and what they were
getting at. And yet she started pouring out her soul to you."

"She was aware of everything," Alexander observed. "She
was aware of why we came and what we wanted of her. She
understood. But she was not talking with the dark side of
our human selves. She ignored the dark side, communicating
only with what was bright in each one's heart. And that way
she changed all of us. After all, I'm an academic. I've done a
lot of work in psychology."

"So, another academic, eh? So what good is all your study
if your thoughts are so slow to catch up?"

"Well, you see, life often happens to deal out its events to us
faster and more accurately than we can handle them. Besides,
Anastasia turned out to be... No, I'm afraid to put her into a
category, any more than that other experience..."

"What other experience?"

"How can I put it? You know? Those old people from
that remote taiga village — well, they're still coming at us.
Together with the frail little girl out in front of them, carrying the thin stick."

"What? Where?"

"They're coming at us, they're coming at all of us who were there and saw them. I thought that this was happening just with me — as soon as I close my eyes, I see them straight off, and sometimes they appear whenever I do anything which, in their opinion, is probably unwarranted. I thought this was happening just with me — but I've been talking with others in the group. Similar things have been happening with the ones who were there."

"But that's all just in your minds, in your imagination."

"What's the difference? We still have to retreat before their advance, even in our minds."

"What could be so frightening about helpless and unarmed oldsters? What are you afraid of?"

"I really don't know what there is to be afraid of. Maybe our own... Maybe we've overstepped some line of permissiveness?"

"What kind of line would that be? That sort of fantasising can drive one crazy. Maybe you just have to think things through as you're doing them, before it's too late."

"Maybe, think things through in time... We all have to think things through."

"And where did you get the notion that after her conversation with Anastasia the little girl's destiny changed, and her mother's too? And the destiny of the other villagers?"

"I told you, I'm into psychology. As an academic I can say this: Anastasia completely changed Aniuta's whole internal programme.

"After being abandoned to the care of her grandparents, the little girl had been spending her time sitting sick and helpless in a corner of a dirty hut, waiting for her mother to come. They kept assuring her that her Mamochka would come and play with her and bring her presents. They did this, thinking they were doing a good deed by lying. In the meantime her mother in the city went on a drinking binge to relieve her feeling of hopelessness. The false assurances had condemned the girl to a state of fruitless expectancy.

"We too sometimes sit around waiting for a dispensation from above. Someone is supposed to come along and make us happy and change our destiny. Maybe that's why we act so lethargically or don't act at all. We don't reflect on the fact that we already have more than enough, and that maybe we should be greeting the one coming with gifts of our own.

"Anastasia changed destiny and the future with her simplicity and sincerity. Just think, the simplest human words can change destiny.

"I've listened to the recording of Anastasia's conversation with Aniuta many times. I have an idea if anyone else spoke that way to the girl, it would have had the same effect. It doesn't actually take much to speak the way she did. The main thing is not to lie. One need only have the sincere desire to help. And helping doesn't just mean sympathising. You have to be free of doctrines of karma, of predestination or, rather, rise above them.

"Of course one can do a lot of talking about karma, the hopelessness of inevitable predestination and what it means for a sick little girl, but Anastasia rose above this sense of inevitability. She simply didn't pay any attention to it. And any other person could do the same. After all, everything was done with words, simple words we use every day. Only they need to be spoken at the right time and in the right place, and in the proper order. It is quite possible that the purity of thought Anastasia talks about causes these words to automatically fall into place in the right sequence, and that is why they are so powerful."

"Well, Alexander, those are all theories of yours, assumptions. You still have to look at real life and see whether any destinies will change on account of a bunch of words or not. Anyway, what could possibly change in life for that little girl? Unless some sort of miracle happened."

"A miracle *has* happened. It turns out that all the miracles we need are within ourselves."

"What kind of miracle happened?"

"Little Aniuta's whole mind and life got reprogrammed. She broke all the bonds of karma for herself and those around her."

"What do you mean, 'broke'? How do you know this?"

"I know it. Some time afterward I went back to the village. I decided to offer Aniuta my radio receiver, since hers was too crackly, and set up an antenna for it on the roof. So I'm walking along to Aniuta's house and I notice that the boards on the wooden sidewalk have been fixed. Before they were quite decayed, and now all the rotting boards had been replaced with new ones. Wow, I thought, what's all this renovation going on here? I saw Aniuta's granddad sitting on the porch, washing his boots in a pail of water. I said hello to him, and explained why I'd come.

"'Well, fine!' said the grandfather. 'Come on in, if you like. Only you'll have to take off those shoes of yours. You see, we've got new rules around the place.'

"I took off my shoes on the porch and accompanied the grandfather into the hut. Everything was simple inside, as you'd expect in a small village, only extremely clean and cozy.

"'You see, our granddaughter's got this new order set up for us,' the grandfather told me. 'She worked at it for a long time. She cleaned the floor, and then washed everything spic and span. She was at it from morning 'til night for over a week, like a wound-up spring. She would have a rest and then start cleaning again. She persuaded me to paint the walls a fresh coat of white.

"'And now when I come into the hut with my boots on and leave tracks, right away she gets out a rag and starts cleaning away the tracks. So, I guess, it's better not to leave any tracks. We don't have any slippers.[1] Instead of slippers she adapted some old galoshes. Here, you can put these on. Make yourself comfortable.'

"I sat down at the table. It was covered with an old, but clean tablecloth. The cloth was torn in one place, and the tear was patched, as neatly as a child's hand could make it, with a piece of coloured cloth cut in the shape of a bunny-rabbit. In the middle of the table stood a cut-glass tumbler, out of which corners cut from notepad sheets neatly protruded — instead of serviettes.

"'I see they've started improving your village, too,' I said to the grandfather. 'And it looks like the authorities have been paying attention, seeing they fixed the wooden sidewalks.'

"And he replied:

"'It's got nothing to do with the authorities. They don't pay any attention to us. It's my granddaughter, Aniuta. She just can't keep still.'

"'What do you mean, Aniuta? She's still a wee one, much too little to repair sidewalks. Those are heavy boards there.'

"'Heavy boards. Yeah. You see, one day I was about to set out hunting, and I asked a neighbour if she would look in on Aniuta. And Aniuta says to me, "Go on, Grandpa, go on about your business. Don't worry, I'll take care of everything myself. Just let me take a saw to that board that's standing against the wall in the barn."

"'I was surprised, but I thought: why not let the child play, if that's the way she likes to play. So I put the board on the wood-block, handed her a couple of saws and set off to do some hunting. Later my neighbour told me what happened while I was gone.

[1] *slippers* — It is customary for Russian hosts to offer their guests slippers to wear during their visit.

"'Aniuta pulled out the old rotten pieces of board from the sidewalk. She measured the hole with a string and began sawing the board I had given her according to the measurement. The neighbour says she spent half the day sawing the board, but she managed to do it somehow. Then she lugged the new board right up to the sidewalk and put it in the place of the rotten one.'

"'She's so thin and frail, how on earth could she have lugged such a heavy board?' I asked.

"'She found herself a helper. Back a couple of months ago she made friends with an orphaned dog, a Siberian laika.[2] An old lady died who lived at the other end of our village, leaving a large dog. Back at the funeral Aniuta kept stroking him. Then she started taking him something to eat. At first the laika wouldn't leave his own yard, even though there was nobody left living in the hut. The old lady had been living alone.

"'Aniuta fed the dog for several days. He started following the girl around, and now he never leaves her side. Now this old dog helps carry out whatever our granddaughter fancies. So he helped her lug the board over. Aniuta tied a string around one end and started in dragging it herself, when the huge dog grasped hold of the other end with his teeth, and between the two of them they managed to drag it to the sidewalk.

"'Then Aniuta asked a neighbour lady for some nails, and borrowed my hammer. And here she was trying to nail the board into place with the hammer. But nothing happened. The neighbour saw Aniuta sitting on the sidewalk, trying to hammer in the nail. She hit her hand in the process and blood started oozing out. The dog was sitting right beside her, watching and whimpering.

---

[2] *laika* — the name given to a number of Arctic breeds of dog, akin to the Canadian husky, trained for pulling sledges and hunting in the North. The word has the same root as the Russian for *to bark* and is commonly used in Russian as a personal name for a dog.

"'The neighbour came over, took the hammer and nailed the board in place. The next evening she saw Aniuta and the dog dragging another board over. Which meant there was another hole in the sidewalk to patch up.

"'The neighbour asked Aniuta if she were going to patch up all the holes this way — couldn't she think up some other little girl's thing to do? And my granddaughter replied:

"'"It's very important, Auntie, for all the sidewalks outside the houses to be new and free from holes. You see, otherwise someone might decide to come visiting, walking along the boards, and there's holes in them, and that would spoil the visitor's good mood. And my Mamochka, when she comes, might get upset if she saw such a shoddy sidewalk."

"'So the neighbour hammered down the second board for her. And then she raised a hue and cry throughout the village, shouting out to everyone: "Get busy fixing the sidewalks in front of your houses. I'm not going to let a child do drudgery on account of your disorderliness! She's working her hands to the bone!"

"'So, you can see, everyone's fixed up the sidewalk in front of their houses. So they wouldn't have to hear the neighbour lady rail at them any more.'

"'And where is your granddaughter now?' I asked the old fellow.

"'She's lugged a tin of paint over to the house at the far end. She'll probably spend the night there, with the old Losin couple. Yeah... She may spend the night there.'

"'What kind of paint, and what's it for?'

"'Just ordinary oil-based paint, bright orange. She got it from the steamship in exchange for fish. That's her latest fancy.'

"'And what kind of fancy might that be?'

"'She's decided that all the huts need freshening up. Need to look more cheerful. So when the ship comes —

that's the ship that collects fish that's been caught around here, she goes and offers 'em a whole catch of fish in exchange for paint. And then she lugs the tin of paint to one of the huts. She asks them to paint the *nalichniks*.[3] And the old people start painting. Soon it'll be my turn. Whaddya know! I'll do the painting. Why not? Maybe it'll be better if the painting gets done, if the huts are going to look more cheerful on the outside.'

"'And where does she get the fish from?'

"'She catches them herself. Every morning she brings home two or three connies,[4] sometimes more. If only once she'd come home empty-handed, but no, the fish just seem to land on her hooks all by themselves. And here I'm lying in bed with my back problems, and she says to me: get up. And keeps at me: "Get up, Grandpa! You've gotta salt the fish, so it doesn't go bad." Every morning it's the same,' the old fellow muttered, but with no trace of annoyance in his voice.

"So I asked him how Aniuta managed to cope with the fishing tackle — all by herself?

"'See, I told you,' he replied. 'Aniuta's got a helper — this Siberian laika. He may be old, but he's smart, and obedient. He helps her carry out all her fancies. Aniuta takes my throw-line with its five hooks, neatly arranges the bait on the hooks and goes down to her treasured spot on the riverbank every evening with her laika. She'll tie one end of the line to a post on the shore, then attaches the other end to a stick. The dog then takes the stick in his mouth and swims out into the river. He keeps on swimming as long as Aniuta, standing

---

[3]*nalichnik* — an ornately decorated board (with carved symbols to repel evil spirits) covering the cracks between the window-frame and the wall, to keep out the elements; nalichniks are a common feature of Russian rural houses.

[4]*connies* (Russian *belorybitsa;* Latin: *Stenodus leucichthys*) — a freshwater white fish, otherwise known as *inconnu* or *sheefish.*

on the shore, keeps encouraging him: "Swim, Druzhok, swim, Druzhok!"[5] The dog keeps pulling the line until Aniuta changes the tone of her voice as she calls: "Come here, Druzhok, come here, Druzhok!" Then the dog releases the stick from his jaws and swims back to shore…

"'Well, that's enough for now. Let's get some sleep.'

"With that the old fellow climbed onto the stove.[6] And I lay down on the wooden sofa. When I woke up at dawn, I went outside and saw Aniuta down by the river tugging on the iron ring to which the fishing line was attached. A huge Siberian laika was helping her. The laika had grasped hold of the ring with his teeth and braced himself with his legs as he backed up. Together they were dragging the line with quite a decent catch on the end of it. Aniuta was wearing rubber boots three sizes too big over her bare feet.

"Once the catch was almost at the shore, she took hold of a scoop net and ran down to collect the fish. The laika was standing on his hind legs, holding the ring in his teeth. Aniuta went into the water deeper than her boots allowed, and the water started pouring over the tops of her boots.

"She drew the catch onto the riverbank and unhooked three splendid fish, which she put into a bag. Then she and the laika together took hold of the rope attached to a piece of plywood carrying the bag, and dragged it home.

"The water was sloshing around in Aniuta's boots, interfering with her walking. She stopped and took off her boots — first one, then the other — and stood barefoot on the cold ground while she emptied out the water. Then she put on her wet boots again and continued on her way.

[5]*Druzhok* (lit. 'Little Friend') — a popular Russian name for a dog.

[6]*stove* (Russian: *pech*) — The vast majority of Russian huts (*izby*) in rural areas have a furnace-size brick stove in the centre with a flat top where the family sleeps to stay warm during cold nights.

"As the two of them together lugged their morning catch up to the porch, I got a good look at Aniuta's face and was amazed.

"Her cheeks were a rosy red, and her little eyes were sparkling with determination. These, together with the hint of a smile on her face, made her virtually unrecognisable by comparison with the sickly, sallow-skinned little girl I had met earlier. Aniuta set about rousing her grandfather. With a rather loud wheeze he climbed down from the stove and put on a jacket. Then he took a knife and salt and proceed to cut up the fish. In the meantime Aniuta served me tea, and I asked her why she got up so early every morning to bring home the fish.

"'Those fellows on the steamship, on the river, they come and collect our fish,' she said. 'They give me money. And I asked them to bring me paint for the houses in our village. They brought me the paint in exchange for the fish. Along with some lovely material for a dress. For that I gave them all the fish I had caught that week.' And when she said that, she went and fetched a huge piece of magnificent silk fabric.

"'Well, Ania,' I observed, 'I see there's enough here for more than one dress. How come so much?'

"'This isn't for me. I've got it ready as a present for my Mamochka, when my Mamochka comes to see me. And I'm also going to give her a beautiful shawl and a long beaded necklace.'

"Then Aniuta opened an old worn suitcase and pulled out a pair of imported women's pantihose, a pearl necklace and a magnificent brightly-coloured shawl.

"'I don't want Mamochka to be upset that she can't give me any presents. I can buy everything for her now myself. I don't want her to think she's been wasting her life.'

"I watched as she joyfully showed me the gifts she had prepared for her mother — she was so happy admiring them — and

I realised what had happened: here Aniuta had transformed herself from an utterly helpless, pitiful little girl, waiting for somebody else to help her, into an active, self-confident individual. And happy that she has known such great success, or maybe her happiness stems from an entirely different source...

"Now I believe that each one's happiness lies within themselves, within each one of us. It is there at a particular level of awareness. The only question is: how do we reach that level?! Anastasia helped little Aniuta reach it. Will she be able to help everyone else do the same? Or maybe we ourselves need to learn in some way how to figure things out ourselves."

Alexander fell silent, and we each became absorbed in our own thoughts.

I wrapped myself in a short thick coat and laid my head against a log. I began looking up at the bright northern stars, and it seemed they were quite low overhead and were also being warmed by the flames of our fire. I tried to go to sleep.

After about three hours' sleep, at dawn Alexander and I headed for the motorboat. But before casting off, Alexander suddenly announced:

"I've been thinking. Now I'm certain. It's not worth your while going into the taiga. You won't find Anastasia there now. Nobody can find her, including you."

"Why not?"

"Anastasia's gone. She's gone deep into the taiga. She couldn't help leaving. If you try to go after her, you might get killed. You're not suited to the taiga. Besides, you've got to write some more. To fulfil your promise to her."

"In order to write more, I've got to hear her answers to the many questions from my readers. Questions about children, about different religions..."

"Nobody'll find her now."

"Why do you keep parroting: 'She can't be found! She can't be found!' I know where her glade is, I'll find her."

"I tell you, you won't. Anastasia can't help but realise that there are people out to hunt her down."

"What do you mean, they're out to hunt her down? Is somebody bribing the local hunters? Just like they pay you and Yegorych?"

"Me and Yegorych? No way! We try to persuade people not to interfere with her, not to alarm her. And if that doesn't work, we take them and let them off on the opposite shore. The local hunters can't be bribed; they've got laws and values of their own. They knew about Anastasia long before you came along. They've always treated her with great respect. They've been careful even when speaking about her amongst themselves. They don't like it when strangers show up in the taiga, and they're pretty good shots."

"Then who could possibly hunt her down?"

"I think: whoever has led us into the condition we find ourselves in at this moment. And is still leading us."

"Can you be more specific?"

"Each one of us has to work that out more specifically on their own."

"But still, who do you have in mind? Someone like Boris Moiseevich?"

"He's just a tool. There's something we can't see that's playing with us. And Boris Moiseevich is starting to realise that now. And maybe the one who hired him has realised it, too."

CHAPTER ELEVEN

Who are we?

"A month ago Boris Moiseevich returned to these parts," Alexander told me. "This time he had no assistants or guards with him. He looked me up. He was quiet and pensive. He and I talked for a whole day. It wasn't so much a conversation as a confession on his part — it wasn't me he was confessing to, of course, but to himself. He gave me a copy of his report on his contact with Anastasia. I copied out some excerpts for you. Would you like me to read them?"

"Who commissioned the report?"

"I don't know. Even Boris Moiseevich doesn't know. He had a meeting with whoever it was in an opulent salon with a fireplace. His sponsor identified himself as a representative of the 'International Academy'. But so many academies have sprouted up recently, it's hard to tell which of them are the really serious ones. Now people have begun judging the seriousness of an organisation by the amount of funding it gets.

"The sponsor hadn't scrimped on the financing. He'd paid for the whole trip right off in cash, and promised not only a substantial bonus but also the future involvement of the whole unit Boris Moiseevich headed in a serious scientific project connected with Anastasia.

"When Boris Moiseevich met with him upon his return to Moscow and presented his report, the sponsor took only a cursory look at it. No doubt he had already been informed of its contents. He threw the report into the fireplace and said to Boris Moiseevich:

"'You were supposed to establish contact with "Object X", as you yourself referred to Anastasia. In carrying out the project you employed not only your own scientific methods and techniques of persuasion, but also violence. The violence was your own initiative.

"'We have decided to double your fee for organising the expedition, and at the same time cancel our agreements with you for any future activity. Here, take your money,' he said, pointing to a briefcase standing beside his chair, 'and forget about the whole thing.'

"Boris Moiseevich tried to explain that the violence had erupted spontaneously, and that he himself found the whole episode quite distasteful, and he realised what harm his group's inexpertness had inflicted on future contacts with Anastasia, and for that reason he would not take any fee at all.

"At that point the man sitting by the fireplace got up from his chair and in a tone that brooked no contradiction, articulated:

"'You *will* take it. And you'll leave. You didn't care about the cause, only the money. So here, take it. We don't need you any more.'

"Boris Moiseevich took the briefcase with the money and left the spacious office salon. He tried to share the money in equal amounts among the members of the expedition, but not all of them accepted it. It only seemed to emphasise the tremendous feeling of unpleasantness at what had been wrought by the participants."

"How come you only copied out excerpts of the report for me?" I asked Alexander.

"Judging by your book, you don't really fancy reading documents filled with terms you don't understand. I tried to copy out only the important points, and places where there wasn't too much specialised terminology."

"So, what do they say about Anastasia?"

Alexander pulled some printed pages out of his pocket and began reading them to me:

Object X cannot be studied by traditional scientific research methods known to us today.

The evaluation criteria currently accepted in scientific circles inevitably posit particular frameworks which automatically exclude properties hitherto unknown and the possibility of encountering phenomena arising out of and connected with isolated situations and the changing psychological state of Object X.

As an information source in various areas of scientific research, the 'object' may prove to have no equal among the sources currently known to science.

The object is most likely not an information carrier in itself. It is not interested in simply receiving and analysing information. However, should there arise a particular goal — and, consequently, a desire — which it deems significant, information accrues to it in a form selected by an unknown entity and in the required amount, for which Object X may instantly find a practical application.

Our group was able to offer only a few hypotheses. But we did confirm experimentally a number of Object X's sayings regarding plants. We were able to establish the existence of the ray. The scientific terms *torsion field* and *radiowave emissions* are not really suitable here. If they are used at all, it is only because there are no other more suitable terms.

The most incredible and doubtful hypothesis, in our view, was the possibility of infusing the text of the book[1] with hidden combinations and signs — according to Object X's terminology — of "the depths of eternity and the infinity

[1] *the book* — i.e., *Anastasia,* Book 1 of the Ringing Cedars Series.

of the Cosmos". The object affirmed that these signs may have a beneficial effect on people.

We were recommending conducting a series of experiments, comparing the parameters of the physiological changes in human beings before and after the reading of the book, with the help of measuring devices used in medical practice. This does not make much sense any more.

Already we are compelled to confirm that the fact of their existence is indisputable. These changes are not effected through the material, physiological organs of the body, but at some intangible, non-material level of society as a whole.

One has the impression that within the milieu of the community of people living on the Earth a reaction is beginning to take place which we are not in a position to arrest — or, for that matter, even to control.

The basic evidence of such a reaction is the psychic response observed in those who have come in contact with the book. Questionnaires, along with examination and analysis of readers' correspondence attest to the fact that a majority of readers have experienced a creative urge expressed in the form of poetic compositions, sketches and drawings, along with the writing and performing of songs. Many readers have felt the impulse to make contact with and cultivate plants, or to change their profession. In certain cases the reading of the book is followed by a significant improvement in one's sense of well-being and the disappearance of symptoms of disease.

We conducted an experiment on thirty people having various ailments. In a psychotherapy/sleep-therapy unit they were asked to read the text of the book. In the case of 27 of them an emotional concentration was observed, along with lack of sleep and an increased hæmoglobin count in the blood. If we assume that the reaction on the part of these readers is due to the vividness of the image of literary art, one can confirm that in terms of psychological effect this particular image far surpasses, by several degrees, all those hitherto known, including classical and biblical images.

The indisputability of such a conclusion is confirmed by the percentage of readers who have expressed their relationship to the book in poetic and other creative forms — according to our statistical survey, this has happened with as many as one in every nineteen readers.

Moreover, it should be noted that the author's expository style is primitive to the extreme. It does not follow any established norm of the literary arts, and the text is replete with grammatical errors. But a computer analysis of the book's readability shows that it has a readability rating of 80% or higher!

In our direct contact with Object X we noticed a phenomenon encountered nowhere else before and with no counterpart in any data observed or recorded by ufologists.

We observed a spheroid energy mass, resembling large ball lightning. Its energy potential far surpasses existing scientific concepts of the power of natural energies. Its ability to change the Earth's gravitational field in a specific location affords it the possibility of instantaneously transforming anything not rooted in the ground into cosmic dust.

During the period of our contact, the Earth's gravitation was changed slightly, but with any increase in its power output we and all material objects might have simply found ourselves somewhere out in space. By contrast, the gravitational field around Object X was not changed, which attests to the possibility of selective influence.

It was evident that the change in the Earth's gravitational attraction was preceded by a reduction in the blue spectrum of natural light.

One could hypothesise that the so-called gravitational attraction of the Earth is not dependent on the Earth itself but on the pressure of light emanating from certain celestial objects, energies, or the Earth's atmosphere as created by an intelligent being.

Despite its ability to acquire large quantities of information, Object X does not attempt to subject it to analysis. It processes the information it receives on the level of feelings and intuition, from which arises an impression of naïvety. The interrelationships between Object X and the energy mass are simple and commonplace, established on the basis of feelings, with no trace of servility or idolisation. They are characterised by full freedom of action in a context of mutual respect.

The luminous energy mass we observed possesses intelligence and, even more incredibly, feelings, something which ufologists have not noted in connection with a single UFO. This is evidenced by the fact that during contact with Object X the rays of the energy mass stroked its feet and hair, and that the mass itself, through its movements, reacted to Object X's emotional state.

Along with the capability of exerting a physiological effect on matter, the phenomenon perceived by us also has the capacity to produce a psychological effect.

It may be hypothesised that Object X may represent an earthly human being who is periodically contacted by representatives of an extra-terrestrial civilisation, or that it is in communication with some kind of natural phenomenon which does not lend itself to scientific investigation.

It may be further hypothesised that Object X itself represents an extra-terrestrial civilisation. However, the object's own declaration: "I am Man, I am a woman" contradicts this hypothesis. Such a declaration places us in an unresolvable dilemma, as the question inevitably arises: "Who then are we?" Or to put it another way: "Has mankind been treading a path of progress or regression?"

CHAPTER TWELVE

Man-made mutants

"Okay, that's enough," I interrupted Alexander. "For me, Anastasia is just a recluse. Maybe she's got some unusual abilities, but I would say she's human, she's Man. Let's hope so, anyway. If I think about everything too much, I could go nuts. So start up that old rattletrap motor of yours and let's go."

It took us about four hours to get to the remote settlement. After I had set foot on the familiar stretch of shoreline, Alexander also got out of the boat and once again tried to persuade me:

"Anastasia's gone, Vladimir. Really give it some thought — you can still change your mind about trying to reach her glade. You won't make it."

"I'm going." I was hoisting my backpack to sling it over my shoulder when I suddenly noticed Alexander unsheathing a large hunting knife.

I threw the backpack down and rifled about on the ground for something I could defend myself with. But Alexander, having bared his right arm to the elbow, suddenly slashed his own arm with the knife and covered the gushing blood with a white linen scarf he had. Then he asked me to fetch the first-aid kit from the motorboat and bind his wounded arm. I did this, still in a state of bewilderment. He handed me the bloodsoaked scarf, saying:

"Tie this around your head."

"What for?"

"At least that way the hunters won't touch you. They will not fire at a wounded man."

"You think those hunters of yours are dumb or something? They only have to come close and they'll see right off it's a prop."

"They won't come close. Why take the chance? They've all got their own territories and pathways. If someone needs to go into the taiga for a good reason, he'll talk to the hunters first, tell them about himself and what he intends to do, and co-ordinate his route with them. If they think he has a good reason, they'll help him, give him advice and may even provide an escort. But they know nothing about you. They may shoot first and ask questions later, but they won't fire at a wounded man."

I took the bloodsoaked scarf and tied it around my head.

"I guess I'm supposed to say thank you, but somehow I don't feel like thanking you."

"No need to. I didn't do it for thanks. I just wanted to do at least something for you. When you get back, light a fire on the riverbank. I'll be passing close by from time to time, and if I see the smoke I'll come pick you up — if, that is, you manage to get back."

As I was walking along, I noticed a couple of dogs about a hundred metres away. Probably from the settlement, I thought. I wished they would come closer, as dogs had a quieting effect on me. I even tried to attract their attention, but they didn't approach, only kept a parallel course to mine. And so we went deeper into the taiga.

It was pointless for Alexander to try and scare me, I thought. The taiga didn't seem hostile to me at all. Maybe it was because I knew at the back of my mind that here amidst the trees and moss-covered logs lived Anastasia, and even if she was strange, she was still a kind person. I held to the notion that here in the taiga with all its tangled undergrowth, its sounds and air so unfamiliar to city-dwellers, lived my very own son. This thought made the taiga feel just a bit more like home to me.

The twenty-five kilometres from the riverbank to the glade presented much more of a challenge than walking along an ordinary road, since there were fallen trees to climb over and thickets to go around. The time I had been walking with Anastasia I hadn't noticed all these barriers, immersed as we were in conversation. The main thing now was not to lose my sense of direction on account of them, and I began checking my compass more often, all the while thinking: How did Anastasia find her glade with no compass? It certainly didn't look as though there was any kind of pathway.

Stopping to rest after every hour, by noon I got to a shallow stream about two metres wide. Anastasia and I had also forded a stream, I remembered. I decided to go across and stop for some time in a glade just on the other side. I made my way along the trunk of a partly rotted tree which had fallen into the stream. The tree didn't extend all the way across, so after tossing my backpack, I made a jump for the shore. But something happened. My leg fell on some kind of protruding snag and got twisted, or sprained somehow. I felt a searing pain through my whole leg and it even spread to my head. I lay there a few minutes and then tried to get up. I realised I couldn't walk. So I lay there, reflecting on what to do next. I tried to remember what you're supposed to do when you twist or sprain your leg. But I had a hard time remembering, probably because the pain was so intense. Then I decided I would lie still for a while, have a bite to eat, and maybe the pain would go away. If need be, I would light a fire and spend the night there. Maybe by morning my leg would even be better. After all, everything with Man heals itself eventually.

It was at this point that I caught sight of the dogs again. There were four of them now, and two more on the other side. And they weren't going anywhere. They took up their positions on either flank, about ten metres from me. The dogs were of various breeds: one was an Airedale, another was a Boxer, the remainder were mongrels. And there was a little lap-dog among them. Their coats were ragged, they were terribly thin, the Airedale's eyes were festering. I remembered hearing my captain's first mate telling about dogs like this. And my sudden awareness of the precariousness of my situation made even the pain in my leg disappear temporarily.

The first mate of my headquarters ship told how people who didn't want their pets around any more would take them off somewhere and abandon them. If they dropped them off within the city limits, the cats and dogs would hang around various scrap-heaps and at least get a little something to keep them going. When dogs were taken out to a remote area, far outside of town, they would group together in gangs and get their food by attacking a living creature. Including people, especially people all by themselves.

These dogs are actually more frightening than wolves. They'll lie in wait for a wounded or exhausted victim and then attack their prey simultaneously. Another thing that makes these gangs of homeless mad dogs more frightening than wolves is their superior knowledge of human habits and their hatred of human beings. They have it in for *people*. They have no experience hunting for wild game, but people are their prey.

It's especially frightening when the gang includes at least one dog who's been trained to attack human beings. I once had a dog, which I took to a private obedience school. The training programme included attacking a person on command. The instructor's assistant would put on a padded coat with long sleeves and the dog would be taught to attack him viciously. If the dog carried out the command properly, he would be rewarded with a treat. They sure went through their paces, those smart-asses!

I wonder if there is any other creature on Earth, apart from Man, that finds it necessary to teach another species to attack one of the teacher's own kind.

The dogs around me began to tighten their circle. I needed to show them, I thought, that I was still alive, that I could move about and defend myself. I picked up a short stick and chucked it at the closest mangy bitch. It managed to dodge the stick and take up a new position. There weren't any other sticks within reach. Then I got a couple of tins of preserves out of my backpack. As I was getting them, the smallest of the gang — the lap-dog — stole up from behind, tore a piece out of my trouser-leg with its teeth and then jumped back. The other dogs watched — probably to see my reaction.

I took one of the tins and chucked it at the nearest large pooch; the other I threw at the lap-dog. There was nothing else to throw. My consciousness was overwhelmed with a sense of hopelessness.

I began imagining how the dogs would tear apart my body and eat it in pieces and how I would still be conscious for some time and witness it all and writhe in pain, since the dogs wouldn't be able to finish me off all at once. And I had nothing with me to bring on a quick death and escape extended torture.

One thing I felt especially bad about was that I wouldn't be able to deliver my backpack containing the gifts for Anastasia from my readers, along with various kiddie items a young child would need.

Half my backpack was taken up with readers' letters full of questions and requests. A lot of letters. Most unusual letters. They wrote from the heart, they wrote about their lives, and there were lots of poems. Maybe not too professionally crafted, not always rhyming, but still there was something good about them. And now they would all be lost, rotting away here in the taiga.

And then a thought struck me, out of the blue. I decided to write a note and place it in the plastic bag with the letters. A note! If anyone found my backpack, they could take all its contents and the money too. And they could send the readers' letters back to my daughter Polina. I told her in the note to publish them once there were enough royalties from my book to cover the expense. It would be a crime for so many soul-inspired poems to be lost forever. Many of their authors were likely writing the first poem in their life, something that came straight from their heart. And now the only poem they ever wrote in their life would be lost.

It was quite a challenge writing the note. My hands were trembling. From fear, most probably. And just why does Man cling so tight to life even in a situation where it is absolutely clear that it's all over? But I managed to finish the note and put it in the plastic bag with the letters. I tied the bag tight so moisture wouldn't get in.

And then all at once I noticed that the dogs, which had already come quite close to me, were beginning to execute a rather strange manœuvre. One by one they started crawling *away* from me. Some of them were sitting up on their haunches looking in the other direction, away from me, and then lay down again, as though in ambush. I managed to get up on one leg to take a look and see what had distracted them. And then I saw... I saw how along the stream, with leaps and bounds, came running none other than Anastasia, her magnificent golden hair trailing in the breeze. And her sweeping stride was so utterly beautiful that I completely forgot about my own danger in admiring the scene.

And all of a sudden it hit me: *the dogs!* They were no doubt under the impression that their prey might now be taken from them, and they were getting set to attack the newcomer running so determinedly toward them.

These starving dogs, brutalised by the wilds, would viciously fight for their prey to the end. Anastasia would not be able to do anything about them all by herself. The dogs would tear her apart, and I cried out as loud as I could:

"Stop, Anastasia, stop! Dogs! Wild dogs here! Don't come this way, Anastasia! Stop!"

Anastasia heard me, but didn't let up her bounding stride for a moment. But while she ran she waved her hand in the air. What has she done now? — I thought. The extraordinary phenomenon she could call upon wouldn't be able to help her now.

As quickly as I could I pulled out of my backpack the little glass jars of baby food. I started throwing them at the dogs, trying to attract their attention to myself and away from Anastasia. One of the jars hit its mark, but the dogs paid no attention to my efforts.

No doubt they realised who their real threat was. No sooner had Anastasia entered their circle than the dogs attacked her from all sides at once. And then...

Oh, what a sight it was! You'd have had to see it to believe it. Anastasia transformed all the energy of her run into a spin. All at once she broke her stride and spun about sharply like a top, or a ballerina twirling on stage, only faster. Upon striking Anastasia's rotating body, the dogs flew off in different directions without causing her any harm, but then, once she had stopped spinning, they got ready to launch a new attack.

I crawled over toward Anastasia. She was wearing her short, light-weight dress. If only she'd been wearing her quilted jacket, it would have been harder for the dogs to bite through.

Anastasia got down on one knee. As she knelt there in the circle of the vicious dogs that were half-crazed by hunger, her face betrayed no fear. She looked at me and said briskly:

"Hello, Vladimir! Only do not be afraid. Just relax a little. Let go. Do not worry, they will not do anything to me, these starving little dogs. Not to worry."

Two huge mutts once more launched an attack on Anastasia from either side. Without getting up and without ceasing her talking, a lightning-fast movement of her hands caught each dog in mid-air by its front paw and spun it around. Moving her body slightly to one side, she let the two dogs crash into each other and drop to the ground.

The other dogs had once more taken up a position, no doubt getting ready for a new attack, but this time they stayed put.

Anastasia stood up and swept her hand up into the air. Lowering it, she slapped herself twice on the thigh.

From behind the nearby thickets there suddenly sprang out four mature wolves. There was such determination in their headlong dash that it seemed they would not think to take account of the numbers or strength of the foe before them. They were spoiling for a fight.

The dogs put their tails between their legs and headed off lickety-split. The wolves ran right past me, practically spraying me with their hot breath. Right on their heels a young wolf cub breezed past in a flicker, trying with all his might, in spite of his shorter stride, not to fall behind the pack. When he reached the spot where Anastasia was standing, he suddenly braked with all four paws, and even did a somersault. Then he jumped up and gave two licks to the fresh scratch on Anastasia's bare foot.

Anastasia abruptly grabbed the cub by his torso and hoisted him up in the air.

"Where are you off to?" she said. "It is not your time yet. You are still too little."

The cub began squirming all over in Anastasia's arms and whining like a puppy. He managed to escape — or, rather, she herself let him go. Once more on the ground, the cub gave one more quick lick to Anastasia's scratch and set off to catch up with the pack.

"But why?" I began questioning Anastasia as she headed over to me. "Why didn't you call in the wolves right off? Why?"

Anastasia smiled, and proceeded at once to feel my arms and legs. With her pure, calming voice she said:

"Please do not worry. I needed to show the dogs that Man is always superior to them. The wolves they will fear in any case. But the dogs have begun making attacks on Man. Now they will no longer attack Man.

"Not to worry. I felt your presence and could tell you were coming. I ran to meet you. Why did you take such a risk in coming into the taiga all by yourself? At first I could not find you, and then I guessed you must have set out on your own."

Anastasia ran off to one side and plucked up some kind of grasses. Then she looked in a different place and did the same. She rubbed the grasses between her hands and carefully soothed my sore leg with her moist palms. And she kept talking non-stop:

"It will go away. It will pass quickly. Before you can say 'Jack Robinson'."

I noticed Anastasia frequently used proverbs and sayings, and I asked:

"Where did you pick up these sayings?"

"I sometimes listen to how various people speak. To learn how to express a greater meaning in just a few words. That displeases you?"

"Well, sometimes they're not quite apropos."

"And sometimes they *are*, well, 'propos'? It is good when they are 'propos'?"

"How do you mean, 'propos'?"

"That was your word. I was just repeating it."

"Tell me, Anastasia, is it still a long ways to your glade?"

"You have come halfway. Together we shall get there quickly."

"It probably won't be very quick, as long as my leg hurts like this."

"Yes, it may still hurt a bit longer. Let your leg rest, and I shall help you walk."

Anastasia hoisted the heavy backpack onto her shoulders. Then, turning her back to me, squatted down on one knee and invited me to climb on.

"Take hold of me and climb onto my back." She said this with such briskness and determination that I immediately obeyed, clasping my arms around her neck. Anastasia promptly rose to her feet and skipped off at a sprightly gait. And throughout our journey she kept talking on the run.

"Not too heavy for you?" I asked after some time.

"One's own burdens are light," replied Anastasia, adding with a laugh:

"I'm a horse and I'm an ox, I'm a wench and I'm a jock!"

"Stop. Let me down. I'll try walking on my own."

"But you are not too heavy for me. Why do you want to try on your own?"

"What's that about a jock? 'I'm a wench and I'm a jock', you said?"

"Just another saying. It was not apropos, eh? Did it offend you?"

"It's okay. I simply want to try walking on my own. If you could just carry my backpack a little while longer."

"If you want to walk on your own, you will have to rest your leg at least another hour..." she advised as she gently lowered me to the ground. "You sit there for a bit, I shall return before long." At that Anastasia ran off for a little while on her own. She presently returned with a bundle of various grasses and once more began rubbing them into my leg near my ankle. Then she sat down beside me, and smiled as she slyly eyed my backpack. All at once she asked:

"Vladimir, please tell me, what is in your backpack?"

"Some letters from readers. Also gifts they sent me to give to you. And I've bought a little something for the baby."

"Could you show me the gifts now while we are resting?"

"And will you show me the baby — our son? You're not going to tell me that he can't see me until I've cleansed myself?"

"Fine. I shall show you our son. Only not right away. Tomorrow I shall show you. The first thing you need to do is to learn a bit about how to converse with him. You will learn quickly once you see him."

"Tomorrow's okay."

I undid the backpack and began to take out its contents. First, the gifts for Anastasia. She took each item carefully in her hands and looked at it with interest, caressing it. She started playing on the Valdai Bells[1] — a present from Olga Sidorovna.[2] And when I handed her a beautiful large, colourful shawl — a gift from another very kind woman, Valentina Ivanovna, I realised right off: women are women, and they all have a lot in common.

Anastasia took the shawl and turned it over in her hands. Then she performed a whole series of manipulations with it. She tied the shawl around her head just like in the picture on the *Alionushka* chocolate bar label,[3] and then in other variations as well.

Then, with a laugh, she tied the shawl around her waist in gypsy fashion, before throwing it over her shoulders and

[1]*Valdai Bells* — popular bronze bells made in Valdai (in north-western Russia on the route between Moscow and St Petersburg). According to legend, these bells date back to the 15th century. They were often used on Russian sleighs pulled by a fast-moving troika of horses sweeping over the silent snow-covered countryside, and even today are considered a symbol of freedom and happiness.

[2]*Sidorovna* — like *Ivanovna* in the following sentence: a patronymic, not a last name.

parading before me in some kind of folk dance. Then she neatly folded the shawl and placed it over the presents spread out on the grass and said:

"Please, Vladimir, say thank you from me to each person, thank these women for the warmth of their heart that they sent along with each of these things."

"I'll thank everyone I see. But I have nothing more to show you. The remaining things aren't for you. They're for our son. All the things he needs. *You* can't use these things — I'll show them to you on the spot when we get there."

"Why do you not want to do this now? We are just sitting here and resting. I would be most interested in seeing what you have."

I didn't want to show Anastasia right off what I had bought for our son, since I remembered what she had said back the first time we met: "You will want to get our son all sorts of senseless toys, but he will not need them at all. You are the one who needs them for your own self-satisfaction, so you can say: 'Oh, look at me, I'm so good and caring!'" But then I still decided to show them to her, since I myself was interested in how she would react to the achievements of our civilisation in matters of child-care. I started showing Anastasia the diapers I had brought, explaining how effectively they absorb moisture when the baby wets them, so he doesn't perspire. I told her everything I had seen in the TV commercial. I showed her the baby food.

"You see, Anastasia, this baby food is simply a marvel. It contains all the substances a baby needs — vitamin

---

[3]The chocolate bar is actually called *Alionka* (pron. *al-YON-ka*), rather than Alionushka. The label for this popular chocolate bar, a favourite with Russian children, shows a little girl with puffy cheeks, wearing a shawl tied to cover her head and neck. 'Alionushka' (another diminutive of Aliona), on the other hand, is the heroine of a Russian fairy-tale, not connected with the chocolate bar label.

supplements too. The main thing is, it's so easy to prepare. Just dissolve in warm water, and the food's ready. Got it?"

"I 'got it'."

"Well, now, you see the factory chimneys of our techno-cratic world aren't just blowing smoke for nothing. We've got some factories producing baby food like this, and the packaging for it. You see that beautiful baby pictured on the package, all smiling and rosy-cheeked?"

"I see."

Finally I showed Anastasia my last gift and commented:

"This is a children's construction set. A construction set's not like a senseless noisemaker. It says here it's specially designed to help the child develop. He can build a car with it, like in the picture, or a steam engine, or an aeroplane, or a house. Well, maybe it'll suit our son a little later. Right now, of course, it's still early for him to make sense of what moves and flies and how."

"Why early? He can make sense of all that right now," replied Anastasia.

"You see, the construction set will help him in this," I observed.

"Do you think so? Are you certain about that?"

"I'm not the only one who's certain, Anastasia. There's a whole bunch of scientists and psychologists who study children's mental development. You see, their endorsements are printed right here on the box."

"Fine, Vladimir, fine. Not to worry. You will do everything the way you feel you should. Only I would ask you to take a look first, observe how our son lives. Then you will be able to determine what his first priorities are."

"Right. Whatever you say." I was glad that Anastasia did not argue with the need for the things I'd brought. I would be able to have a look for myself and decide.

"In the meantime let us hide your backpack here," she said.

"Then, once you determine what thing is needed first, I shall run and fetch it, or I shall fetch the whole backpack if necessary. Right now it is heavy to carry. Your leg still hurts after all, and you do not wish me to carry you."

"Well, okay, let's hide it for the time being," I agreed. "Only we'll take the letters with us. There are a lot of questions in them for *you*. I didn't memorise them all."

"Fine, we shall bring the letters," Anastasia agreed, taking the package. Once she had hid my backpack in a safe place, I leaned my arm on her shoulder, and the two of us headed off in the direction of her glade.

It was late at night by the time we arrived.

As before, the glade was empty. No structures, not even a lean-to. But somehow I got the feeling that I had come home. Even my mood was uplifted, and a sense of calm had set in. I felt like going to sleep. Probably because I had been talking all the previous night with Alexander. Wow! I thought — there's absolutely nothing in this glade, and yet I get the feeling I've come home.

Evidently, one's sense of home is not in the size of one's living space or even a castle, but in something else.

Anastasia at once took me to her lake and recommended I bathe. I really didn't feel like bathing, but I thought I should be obedient to her in everything, at least for now, so I'd get to see my son sooner.

When I came out onto the shore after bathing, it was colder than in the water. Anastasia dried me off with the palms of her hands, wiped me with some kind of grasses, and my body began to feel warm, even hot. Then she handed me her dress and said with a laugh:

"Please put it on, Vladimir. It will be like a night-shirt for you. I shall soak and wash your clothing, which has a strong odour coming from it."

I put on Anastasia's dress. I knew the odour must be elimi-nated, and that was that.

"So our son won't be scared off?"

"For him too," Anastasia replied.

"But it'll be cold for me to sleep in nothing but a dress."

"Not to worry, I have already arranged everything. You will have a good night's sleep, and you will not be cold. You can put the packet with the letters under your head for a pillow. I have thought of everything — you will have a good night's sleep, and you will not freeze."

"With the bear to keep me warm again, eh?... I will not sleep with a bear. I'll manage somehow on my own."

"I have made up your bed so that you will not be too cold or too hot."

We went to the dugout where I had slept before. Anastasia pushed aside the branches hanging over the entrance. I caught the pleasant aroma from the dried grasses, and crawled into the dugout, lay down amidst the grasses, and felt the sleep of sweet languor envelop me all around.

"You can cover yourself with my cardigan, but even without it, you will still not be cold. If you wish, I shall also lie down beside you and keep you warm." I heard Anastasia's words through a half-sleep and responded:

"No need. You'd better go to our son, keep him warm..."

"Not to worry, Vladimir. Our son is already capable of han-dling a great deal on his own."

"How can he do things on his own? He's still too young..." But that was all I could say. I was already immersed in a deep and calm, blissful sleep.

Chapter Thirteen

A new morning — a new life

I woke in the morning. I felt in such an extraordinarily good mood that I just lay there thinking I'd better not budge for the time being, lest the good mood suddenly vanish. What kind of a night did I have, anyway? And why did I get the impression in the morning that over the past night my whole body and consciousness were literally bathed in love? By the light of day it became clear to me why I had felt neither too cold nor too hot during the night. I was lying immersed in dry grasses and flowers, which gave off a pleasant warmth and aroma.

Readers often ask how Anastasia keeps from freezing in the wintertime, during the cruel Siberian frosts, but it's really all so simple: if you bury yourself in a haystack, there are no frosts to fear. Granted, she has some sort of alternative source of warmth, given that she can walk about semi-nude even when it's +5°[1] out and doesn't get cold. She even goes swimming then and doesn't give so much as a shiver when she comes out of the water.

I continued to lie there in the bliss of my dried grasses and thought about how the morning breaking meant a new day had come, and I got the impression as though a new life were beginning. I thought if only this were the way it could be every morning, then in one lifetime one could live a thousand ages, as it were, and each age would be as magnificent as this morning. But how does one make each new day turn out as magnificent as *this* morning?

[1] +5° (Celsius) — approximately equivalent to +40° Fahrenheit.

I didn't get up until I heard Anastasia's cheerful voice calling out to me:

"God surely gives to him who rises early."

I crawled out of my splendid night-time lodgings. Anastasia was already standing right up there at the entrance. Her golden hair was woven into a braid, which was tied with grasses at the end, like a bow. Her new hairdo looked very nice on her.

"Let's go to the lake — you can wash yourself and get dressed," Anastasia proposed, tossing her braid coquettishly to the front.

Well, now, women are women after all, I thought, and said to her aloud:

"That's a very pretty braid you have, Anastasia."

"Pretty, eh? Very, very pretty?" she laughed, as she twirled around.

We ran to the lake. There on the shore, over some branches, were hanging my shirt, trousers, undershirt — in sum, everything I had taken off the night before. I felt them, and they were dry already.

"How did you manage to dry them so quickly?"

"I gave them some help," Anastasia replied. "I put them on myself and ran about a little wearing your clothes, and they dried out very quickly. Now you will be able to put them on after your dip in the lake."

"And are you going to be taking a dip, too?"

"I have already done everything I need to to greet the day."

Before I went into the water, Anastasia rubbed my body down with some sort of paste made from grass. And when I plunged in, the water all around me began to sizzle and my body smarted a little, but when I came out, I felt really refreshed. As though the pores of my skin were starting to breathe with great intensity all by themselves, each one taking in air individually. My overall breathing was free and easy.

Just as she had done the night before, Anastasia, ever cheerful and playful, began once more to rub the moisture off my body with her hands. As she was rubbing my back, I suddenly felt something hot unexpectedly spurt down my spine. It happened once, then again — I turned about sharply and there she was, squeezing her breast with both hands, aiming a stream of warm breast milk right into my face, then from the other breast a stream of milk spurted onto my chest. And then she let loose with a fast rub up and down my body, accompanied by a roar of laughter.

"What are you doing that for?" I asked, when I had recovered from my surprise.

"Because! Because!" guffawed Anastasia, as she handed me my shirt and trousers. They too did not smell the way they did before, and I noticed this as soon as I put them on. Then I said to Anastasia, in a serious tone:

"Okay, I've done everything as you wished. Now let me see our son."

"Fine. We shall go. Only, please, Vladimir, do not try to approach him right off. Watch him for a while at first, try to understand him."

"Fine, I'll watch, okay! And I'll understand."

We went back to the glade which was now so familiar to me. When we reached the bushes at the edge of the glade Anastasia said:

"Let us sit here quietly and watch: he will be waking up now and you will see him."

Beside a tree at the edge of the glade the bear was lying on her side, but I couldn't see any baby. I was getting more and more excited, and my heart started beating strangely.

"Where is he?" I asked Anastasia with bated breath.

"Look more closely," she replied. "Look, you can see his little head and feet sticking out from under the bear's paw. That is where he sleeps, in her groin. It is soft and warm there, and she keeps her paw on top of him — not pressing down, but just to provide a little covering."

And I saw the scene. The boy's tiny body was resting in a cradle of thick bear fur, in the huge beast's groin, under her slightly raised front paw. The bear was lying on her side without stirring, turning only her head from side to side as she looked around. The wee little legs wiggled in the thick fur, at which point the bear raised her paw a little more.

The baby was waking up. When he moved his arm, the bear raised her paw. When his arm dropped back to his side, she lowered her paw a little. Only her paw and head moved. There was not a stir from the rest of her body.

"How can she lie like that without stirring? Isn't it uncomfortable to maintain that one position the whole time?" I asked.

"She can lie like that without stirring for a long, long time. And it is not hard for her at all. She is just so thrilled when he crawls into his little bed. And now she has started to take herself very seriously. She has a sense of responsibility. When the time approached to start a family, she did not even let her intended mate come near her. That is not too good. But when our son grows a little, she will allow her mate to approach her again."

As I listened to Anastasia I couldn't take my eyes off my son — I watched as the little feet once again wiggled beneath the bear's huge paw. Then the paw went up in the air.

The baby moved his arms and legs, stretched himself, raised his head, then all at once stopped moving.

"Why did he stop moving? Is he going to go back to sleep?" I asked Anastasia.

"Look more closely, he is going piddle. The bear did not manage to let him down to the ground on time, or perhaps she did not want to — she really spoils him, you know."

The little fountain kept trickling onto the bear's fur. Like the boy, she too had stopped moving — even her head and her paw — until the fountain had ceased its trickle. Then the bear began to turn over onto her other side, and the baby slid down to the ground.

"All right. You see, she thinks he will go on to do his Number Two, our little Man," Anastasia said cheerfully.

The tiny human body lay on the grass, tensing its abdomen muscles in preparation for his 'Number Two', while above it hovered the enormous bear. It seemed as though the bear was helping the baby along with her rumbling sounds, as if going through a similar preparation herself. The boy turned over on his stomach, started moving his arms and crawling across the grass on all fours. His little bottom had got dirty from his pooping. The bear went over to him and lapped his tiny bottom with her enormous tongue, wiping off the poop, just like a nanny. She gave the boy a push with her tongue, and he plopped on his tummy, but got up again on all fours and went on crawling. The bear followed him and gave his bottom still another lapping, even though it was already clean by now.

"What do you think, Vladimir? Do you think she would be able to take off his dirty diapers or underpants and put new ones on?" Anastasia asked quietly.

"Okay, okay!" I responded, also in a whisper. "I get it."

The boy turned over onto his back, and when the bear persisted in lapping his thighs, he made a nimble move and his little hand latched on to the fur on the bear's muzzle.

In response to what looked to be insignificant movements by the boy's hand, the bear proceeded to rest her huge head on the ground at his feet. He grabbed hold of her muzzle, reached up with his other hand and started climbing up the bear's head.

"Where on earth is he going?" I queried.

"To the bear's eyes," responded Anastasia. "Her eyes sparkle. They fascinate him, and he always wants to touch them."

The boy lay on his tummy on the bear's muzzle and looked at one of her eyes. He then tried touching it with his finger, but all at once her eye snapped shut. The boy's finger poked at her eyelid. After waiting a little while longer and still not seeing any sparkling eye, the boy began climbing down from the bear's muzzle, then crawled a little way across the grass, and stopped to look at something on the ground. The bear got up and roared twice.

"She's calling the wolf. She needs to clean herself up and have something to eat. Now you will see how they have a friendly conversation amongst themselves," Anastasia commented.

A few moments later the she-wolf appeared at the edge of the glade. The bear did not show any signs of welcoming her presence, but greeted her with a threatening roar. The wolf's own behaviour was far from friendly. She surveyed the whole glade. She pranced a bit around the edge, lay down, then took a big leap and lay down again, as though ready to pounce.

"What kind of friendly conversation do you call that?!" I asked. "Why did the bear call her, and then roar at her like that? And the wolf seems pretty threatening herself!"

"That is the way they talk with each other. The bear stopped the wolf with her roar to make sure everything was in order with her. To check that she was not sick with anything, that it was not dangerous to let her approach a child of Man, that she was strong enough to defend him. The wolf showed that she was completely prepared. She showed it by her actions, not with words. You saw how she walked past and jumped pretty high."

Indeed, the bear, after observing the wolf, calmly shuffled off out of the glade. The wolf lay down on the grass not far from the little one. The baby kept staring at something for a while longer, feeling the grass. Then he noticed the wolf and crawled toward her. As he approached, he began feeling her muzzle with his hands, stroking her teeth with his finger, patting her tongue. The wolf lapped his face, at which point little Vladimir crawled onto her stomach, felt the wolf's nipples, sucked his hand all over and screwed his face into a frown.

"Time for our son to eat," Anastasia began speaking again. "But he is not yet so hungry that he will drink the wolf's milk. I am going to leave you for a little bit, while you sit here at the edge of the glade. If he sees you and is interested, he will crawl over to you. Only do not pick him up yourself. He is already a Man, even if small in appearance. He will not understand meaningless cooing sounds. Besides, violence may result if you try to pick him up against his will. He will not understand that. Even if you do it with good intentions, but without his permission, you will make a bad impression on him."

"Right," I said. "I shall not try to pick him up. I'll just sit here like this. But the wolf — she won't touch me?"

"With the scent you have now, she will not touch you."

Anastasia clapped her thigh twice. The wolf got up, turning her head in Anastasia's direction. Then, after a glance at the baby, who had started playing again with some kind of bug, she ran over to Anastasia.

Anastasia came up very near to me. She summoned the wolf to approach closer, then gestured to her to lie down.

"Can I stroke her, to finally make friends with her?" I suggested.

"She will not appreciate any condescending familiarity on your part. She understands everything and will not touch you, but she will not tolerate any display of superiority," Anastasia replied. She sent the wolf back out into the glade and ran off to tend to some affairs of her own, promising to return shortly.

I emerged from behind the bushes, where Anastasia and I had hid ourselves to observe the scene taking place in the glade. I came out and sat down on the grass about ten me-tres[2] from little Vladimir. I sat there that way for about fif-teen minutes. He didn't pay the slightest attention to me. I thought that as long as I continued sitting quietly, he would never pay any attention to me. And so I gave a couple of clicks with my tongue.

The little one turned his head and looked at me. My son! My very own son had his eyes fixed on me with fascination, and I was excitedly looking at him. I could even feel a flush all through my body from the excitement.

I had the urge to run and take his little body into my arms, squeeze him and press him against my chest. But Anastasia's request and (more significantly) the presence of the wolf held me back.

And then my little son began slowly crawling toward me. He kept his eyes fixed on me all the while he was crawling. My heart started beating so loud in my chest that I could hear it — what was it beating like that for? Maybe it would fright-en the little one away, it was pounding so.

But he kept crawling and crawling, and again something in the grass caught his eye, and he began poking around after a little bug. Then he began to examine something crawling along his arm. At this point he was three metres away. My little son had stopped short in his crawling only three metres away from me!

All over some bug. And what kind of world was out there in the grass, what kind of life had taken his fancy so? What kind of order or rules do they have in the forest anyway? Here's this little boy with his very own father right in front of him, and he's more interested in some kind of bug! That's not the way it should be. The child should know that his father is more important than a bug.

---

[2]*ten metres* — approximately equivalent to 33 feet.

All at once the little one looked up again in my direction, showed me a toothless smile, and quickly started crawling again, more nimbly than before. I was all prepared to pick him up, but then noticed that he kept on crawling right past me, not paying any attention to me.

I looked around and saw Anastasia standing all smiles behind me, a little to one side. She sat down and put her hand on the ground, palm upturned. The boy smiled and climbed up to his mother's breast. Anastasia didn't pick him up, but ever so gently helped him climb up, ever so gently helped him reach her breast. Now he was already in her arms, clapping his tiny hands against the exposed breast and smiling at Anastasia. Then, after feeling and stroking her nipple, he closed his lips tight about it and began sucking on the supple breast. Anastasia in the meantime just gave one look at me, putting her finger to her lips to let me know I should keep quiet. I sat there the whole time without uttering a word while she fed our son.

It seemed as though all during the feeding Anastasia was totally oblivious to my presence. Indeed, she did not seem to be aware of the world around her at all. The whole time she concentrated her gaze on our son. And it also seemed as though they were somehow communicating with each other. This impression came from the fact that after sucking for quite a while the baby would suddenly stop, turn away from the nipple and look into Anastasia's face. Sometimes he would be smiling, at other times his face had a serious expression. Then he became very still and slept for a while in his mother's arms. When he awoke, his face once again broke into a smile, and Anastasia sat him on the palm of her hand, supporting his back.

Their faces were very close together, and the baby would feel Anastasia's face with his hands, and press his cheek against hers. Then he spied me once again. And once more he fell still for a while, staring at me in fascination.

All at once he reached out his little hand toward me, inched his body forward in my direction and uttered the sound *eh*. Involuntarily I reached out my hands to him, and at that point Anastasia handed him over to me.

Here I was holding in my arms the tiny body of my very own son — the son I had so greatly desired! Everything else in the world vanished into oblivion. And I had the strong urge to do something for him. The baby felt my face, pressed his lips against it. Then he recoiled with a frown, apparently feeling the prickles on my unshaven face. After that — I don't know how it happened, but I got an uncontrollable urge to kiss his warm little cheek. And I resolved to kiss him! But instead of a kiss I somehow ended up giving his cheek two quick laps, the way the wolf did.

The boy recoiled from me and began batting his eyelids in amazement. Anastasia's loud trills of laughter filled the glade. The baby at once reached out his little hands toward her and started laughing too, squirming in my arms. I realised he was asking to be released. My son was leaving me. Obedient to his will and the established rules of communication here, I carefully put him down on the grass. He immediately crawled over to Anastasia. She jumped up with a laugh, ran around me and sat down on the other side of me, very close. Whereupon the little one turned around and with a big smile crawled over to the two of us. He climbed into Anastasia's arms and once more began to feel my face.

This is how I first communicated with my son.

Chapter Fourteen

A father's role

My son, my little Vladimir, finally fell asleep. After his feeding he played for a while with something in the grass. He felt a cedar cone which had fallen to the ground and tried to lap it. He looked up at the clouds floating by in the sky. He listened to the birds sing, then climbed up a little hill, where the grass was thicker, curled up, closed his eyes, smiled at something, and fell asleep. Anastasia ran off to take care of some sort of tasks of her own. I set out for a walk in the forest alone, immersing myself in thought to the exclusion of everything around me. At the same time I couldn't get rid of the alternating feelings of joy and disappointment.

I sat down under a cedar tree at the edge of the lake and decided to just sit there without moving until I thought of some way that I as a parent could contribute to my child's upbringing. I had to think of something to make him feel his father was the most important thing in his life.

When Anastasia approached, I didn't feel like talking with her at first. It was her laughter, in fact, that had distracted my son from me. Anastasia sat quietly by my side, her hands clutching her knees, thoughtfully contemplating the calm waters of the lake. She was the first to speak.

"Please do not be offended at me. Your communication struck me as so funny. I could not restrain myself."

"That's not what I'm bothered about."

"What is it then?"

"Many readers' letters ask about how to bring up children, they want me to ask you everything about your system of raising children and to describe it in my next book. But what is there here to describe? There is no system — quite the opposite. What you have here is some kind of anti-system. For example, what should fathers do under such circumstances? — a reader might ask."

"You used a most appropriate word — *anti-system* — you can describe that."

"But who would be interested in that? People are looking for practical guides where it tells them what they should do with their baby when he's say, one month old, and then when he's two months old, and so on. An hourly schedule. Books that offer a dietary programme. A complete timetable for bringing up the child according to his age. But here you have only a complete indulgence of the child's whims. An all-permissive attitude."

"Tell me, Vladimir, what do you want our son to be like when he grows up?"

"What do you mean, what do I want him to be like? Of course I want him to be a happy, normal and successful individual."

"And are there many happy people amongst your acquaintances?"

"Happy? Well, if you're talking about completely happy people, I'd have to say: probably not very many. Everybody's got something not quite right with their lives. Either there's not enough money, or they're plagued by illness or family squabbles. But I want my son to avoid any kind of unpleasant experiences."

"Then think about it: how can he avoid them if you deliberately squeeze him into the system everyone is brought up in? And think: might there not be a certain pattern in the fact that all parents want to see their children happy, and yet they grow up and turn out just like everyone else — not very happy?"

"A pattern?" I queried. "What kind of pattern? If you know, tell me yourself."

"Let us ponder this question together."

"This is something people have been thinking about for ages, Anastasia. All kinds of scholars and specialists are pondering it. For this they have invented all sorts of systems of child-rearing, worked out schedules, trying to find the most efficient system."

"Take a more careful look around you, Vladimir. See the trees, grasses and flowers growing. How could one possibly draw up an advance schedule of the days and hours when they should be watered? You would not go watering flowers when they were being washed with water from heaven simply because someone worked out a detailed schedule for watering them."

"Now you're going too far. That's just nonsense — that's not an example for raising children. It's not something that can happen in life."

"But you know, Vladimir, this is exactly what *does* happen in life. No matter what the system. It is still only a system. It is always calculated to wean the heart and soul away from Man when he is still small and to subject him to the system. So that he grows up like everyone else, in a way that will fit the system. And so it goes on for ages on end, so as to prevent the human soul from experiencing clarity of vision. To prevent Man from discovering himself in his beauty as a whole, with a God-given soul. Yes, Man! The ruler of all the Universe."

"Hold on a moment, don't get carried away beyond my reach, speak calmly using everyday speech. What do parents need to do to make it so? So that children will grow up, as you say, with a soul that is free? To be rulers of the Universe, and happy? As God Himself has wished?"

"They must not interfere, they need to see their children clearly in their own thinking the way God Himself has wished. It is the aspiration of all the forces of Light in the Universe that each newborn child be endowed with the very best of creation. It is the parents' duty not to hide the creative Light under the erudition of invented dogmas. For ages upon the Earth debates have arisen as to which system might be the wisest. But think about it yourself, Vladimir. Debates arise where Truth is hid from sight. Fruitless debates can go on forevermore as to what might be found behind the closed door. But one has only to open the door and it will be clear to all, and there will be nothing to debate, since everyone will be able to see the Truth for himself."

"But in the final analysis, who will open this door?"

"It is already open. All that remains is for the eyes of the soul to be opened to see and gain awareness."

"Gain awareness of what?"

"You were asking me about systems. You were mentioning the schedules and everyday régimes and how someone sets them forth for people in books. But think about it: who can tell more clearly about creation than the Creator Himself?"

"But the Creator doesn't tell anything. Up to now He has said hardly a word. Nobody hears His words."

"Words thought up by Man have many meanings. The Creator patiently and lovingly speaks with each one of us through splendid, imperishable acts. The rising of the Sun and the silvery sheen of the Moon, the soft mist and tender dew, playing with the Sun's ray and drinking in the heavenly blue. The Universe is filled with so many clear examples like that. Just look around you. They touch you and everyone else too."

Again, if everything Anastasia said about child-rearing were to be laid out, the result would probably be the complete opposite of how we handle this matter today.

I have already said that Anastasia, along with all her forebears through the ages, treats a newborn as a deity or an immaculate angel. They consider it totally unacceptable to interfere with the child's thought process.

Anastasia's grandfather and great-grandfather were able to observe for long periods at a time how their little grand-daughter would be fascinated by a bug or a flower, or the contemplation of something. They tried their best not to distract her with their presence. They would converse with her only when she herself paid attention to them and showed a desire to communicate. Anastasia maintained that at the very moment I was observing little Vladimir contemplating something in the grass, he was becoming aware not only of the bugs but of all creation.

According to her, a bug is a more perfect mechanism than any manufactured product, let alone a primitive construction set.

A child provided with the opportunity to communicate with these perfect beings will himself become more perfect than through communication with primitive lifeless objects.

Besides, as she maintains, every blade of grass, every bug, is interrelated with the whole of creation and subsequently aids the child in becoming aware of the essence of the Universe and of himself as part of it, to become aware of his innate purpose. Artificially created objects have no such connection and do not arrange priorities and values in the child's brain in the right way.

To my observation that the conditions in which she — and now our son — were being brought up were totally different from those in which children of our civilised world are to be raised, she responded as follows:

"Even in the mother's womb, and especially when a helpless infant, as it seems, is given birth in the world, the forces of Light in the Universe rejoice. They rejoice in the trembling hope that the newly arrived immaculate Godlike Man will become their kind ruler and intensify the Light of Love from the Earth.

"Everything has already been provided for him by the Creator. Through a bug, a tree, a blade of grass, a seemingly ferocious beast, the Universe is prepared to be a good nurse for him. Even in a Man outwardly small we see the great work of the Creator of all. In a burst of bright inspiration Man has been co-created by the Creator. And with his birth has been created for him a Paradise on Earth.

"Nothing and no one has power over the Creator's supreme co-creation. His burst of love and bright inspiration are already comprehended in each engendered moment for the world.

"Of all the beings in the unfathomable Universe only one is capable of influencing his destiny by coming between God, Paradise, a star of happiness and Man."

"So," I queried, "does that mean that there is a being in the world more powerful than God?"

"There is nothing in the world more powerful than Divine inspiration," replied Anastasia. "But there is a being equal to it in power, capable of coming between God — the most tender educator — and the angelic child — Man."

"And who is that, how is he called?"

"That being is *Man the parent*."

"What? But how can it happen that parents can wish unhappiness for their children?"

"Everyone *wants* happiness. But they have forgotten the path to happiness. That is why they are perpetrating violence out of good intentions."

"Can you offer proof, even just a little, of what you say?" I asked.

"You spoke of various systems of raising children," Anastasia responded. "Think about it. There are many systems. But there is only one Truth. And this alone means that the many are leading in the wrong direction."

"How can one tell the true system from a false one?"

"Try to look at life with an open heart. Purify thought from vain and fruitless art, and then you will see the world, the Creator of the Universe and yourself."

"Where are the eyes of the heart, in place of ordinary eyes? Who is capable of discerning all this? Couldn't you talk about things in more specific terms? And in simpler, conversational phrases? You said that your language would be similar to mine, but you are talking differently. And you are making me talk like you. I can sense how you are talking differently."

"Only a wee bit differently. And you will be able to remember the gist of what I say. And my speech will mix with yours. And do not worry, do not feel shy about the combinations of words you use. Your language will be understandable to many people. It will reveal to many hearts the essence concealed in those very hearts. Let the poetry of the Universe express itself in the way you write."

"What's going on here? I don't want anyone to change the way I write."

"But yet you were offended when a journalist called your language 'stilted'. I, along with your readers, can make it so your language may leap from 'stilted' into 'the best-sounding of all time'."

"Well, okay, let's have it that way down the road, but for now I just want to hear simple language. As it is, the issue is so complex, it is incomprehensible. How does it all happen, and how come *parents* are closing off the path to happiness for their children? And is that in fact what is really happening? First of all I have to be convinced that that's really the case."

"Fine. If you want to be convinced, try recalling scenes from your own childhood."

"But that's hard to do. Not everyone can recall things that happened in their infancy."

"And why might that be? Is it not because memory attempts to spare our feelings and excise what is empty and fruitless? It tries to erase any suggestion of hopelessness, to rub out what you experienced in your mother's womb when you sensed the world's verbal abuse through the sufferings of your mother. Do you want me to help you recall the other things?"

"Well, you can give it a try. What other things were there that have gone from my memory?"

"The other things are not things you wish to remember — you are reluctant to remember how you, the ruler of the Universe, lay all by yourself helpless in your crib. You were so tightly wrapped up, it was like being bound in a cocoon, and smiling people decided when you should eat and when you should sleep. You wanted to think everything through for yourself, to make sense of what was going on. But so often they would simply make cooing sounds and toss you up toward the ceiling. But what for? — you never got a chance to think about that. After growing a little, you began to see a great many things around you that had no voice and no heart. But you were not allowed to touch them. You could touch only those things which people handed you. And you resigned yourself to trying to figure out: where was the perfection in any of the joy-toys you were offered? But there was no way you could have found, in this absurd primitive object, what had never been there in the first place and never could.

"But still you kept searching, you did not completely give up — you felt things with your hands, you tried to bite them, but to no avail. You did not find any explanation. That was when you first wavered, you who were born to be ruler of the Universe. You decided that you were unable to decide anything for yourself. You were betrayed by those who gave you birth, and you betrayed yourself."

"You talk about the events of *my* life. Was there anything in which I was different from other kids?"

"I am talking specifically about you. And about those who are listening to me at the moment."

"So that must mean there are many rulers of the Universe, if each one of us is born to be one. But how can *that* be? What sense does it make being a ruler, if there are many ruling over the same thing? Or does that mean there are many universes?"

"There is one Universe. Just one. Indivisible. But in that one Universe each one has his own space, and is responsible for the whole. Each one is responsible."

"So where is it — my space, I mean?"

"It has been lost. But you will find it!"

"When did I manage to lose it?"

"When you gave up."

"What do you mean, I 'gave up'? I was just like all the other kids."

"Like all the other children, you believed in the kindness of people around you, you believed in your parents, you began more and more to repress your own desires. And you accepted their belief that you were nothing but an ignorant, insignificant youngster.

"And the sensations inculcated in you by the abuse of your childhood keep on haunting you throughout your life, even to the point of attempting to reproduce themselves in your offspring. You went to school like everyone else. There you were told how Man was nothing but a monkey. How he was a primitive creature. How foolish he was to believe in God. You were told about how there was just one leader who knew everything. A leader chosen by the people. A leader who alone was more worthy and more intelligent than anyone else. And you got carried away with poems about that leader. You began glorifying him without a second thought."

"It wasn't just that I extolled and read verse as I was told — I actually believed it back then."

"Yes, many people read verse. There were even competitions to see who could extol him better than anyone else. And you tried to be the best."

"So did everyone else back then."

"Yes, the whole system demanded that everyone have the same aspirations. And thereby perpetrated violence on everyone. It tried to break people to preserve itself.

"But then, all at once, part way through your life, you discovered that there were a lot of systems out there and that they were all different. Then you discovered that Man, quite possibly, was never a monkey. And the very wise leader turned out to be a very stupid tyrant. And it turned out that your generation had been living life all wrong. Now there was a new system to live by.

"And then you became a parent. And unthinkingly you handed over your daughter to the new system, as though you were doing her a favour. You were not thinking, as you did before. You used to *wonder* when your toys made noise, but you don't wonder any more. Having accepted abuse yourself as a normal state of affairs, you began abusing your own child. Century after century various systems have come and gone, one after the other, but all with a single goal — to *kill you,* a 'ruler' and wise creator, and transform you into a soulless slave.

"The system always operates through parents. And through those who proclaim themselves to be wise teachers. They will come up with new teachings, thereby engendering a whole new system. And it does not take much investigation to see clearly that they are motivated by the age-old ambition to separate you from God. To come between you and make both you and God try to live and work only for them. This is the core of any system. And you, Vladimir, started asking me to create yet another system. I shall not be able to fulfil your request. You must look around you. Try to make sense of things through your heart alone."

"Tell me, Anastasia, what about our son? Do you mean to say that living out here in the dense taiga, among all the wild beasts, he has not known violence, even in the least?"

"He knows neither violence nor fear. He is ever more confident that everything here is subject to Man and that Man is answerable for everything."

"But wasn't it violence, at least in a small degree, when the bear lapped his dirty bottom after he woke up? When he fell on his stomach after the bear lapped him? And she did this a second time after he began crawling again. And the second time he fell down. The way I saw it, he really didn't like the bear lapping him like that. That was why he grabbed the bear by her muzzle, so she would stop pushing him with her tongue."

"And right at that point the bear *stopped* lapping him. A little later he will realise the significance of this procedure, but right now he sees it as a game. He himself plays with the bear and wants her to chase him."

"You say Man is the wisest creature in the Universe, Anastasia, but here our son is being raised by wild animals. That's not quite normal. I saw one time on TV how they showed a person who was already grown up. As a young lad he had landed among wolves, and when he was grown up people caught him, and it was a long time before he could talk anything like a human being. He seemed quite backward mentally."

"As far as our son is concerned," Anastasia replied, "all the wild animals around do not serve as child-raisers, but rather as good, kind, capable nannies, who sincerely love our little boy. And there is no doubt they would be ready at any moment to give their lives for their little fellow."

"Have you been giving them this kind of training for a long time? Did your grandfather and great-grandfather help you?"

"What need is there for training? Everything was done ages ago by the Creator."

"But how could He have foreseen everything in advance, to be able to teach each creature what to do in any given instance? Back there in the glade, as I was watching, our son was looking at the squirrels, and one in particular caught his fancy. He held out his little hand to it, smiled, and uttered a drawn-out *eh* sound. And the squirrel dashed right over to him — that same squirrel that had caught his eye. The little one then played with it, took it by its paw and stroked its tail. Now how could the Creator have foreseen this particular situation and taught the squirrel what to do?"

"The Creator is wise. He made everything more simple and to perfection."

"How?"

"From a Man who is free from aggression, selfishness, fear and many other dark feelings which came along later, emanates the Light of Love. Even though it is invisible to the eye, it is stronger than the light of the Sun. Its energy is life-giving. The way the Creator arranged things, only Man is endowed with such a tremendous ability. Only Man! He alone is capable of bringing warmth to all living creatures. That is why all living creatures are drawn to him.

"As Vladimir, our little son, was paying attention to the squirrels, he fixed his gaze on one of them in particular, concentrated his attention on it, and his warmth went out to that little squirrel. In this warmth the creature felt a sense of grace, and rushed toward the source, and was delighted to play with him. Our son can summon any animal that way.

"Thanks to the Creator all newborns have such an ability — when they are still in the Space of Love and nothing has yet erased this magnificent element within them. The Space of Love begins with the mother's womb, and then only spreads apace. Only Man is endowed with the power to wreck or perfect this Space.

"My grandfather did train the eagle — you remember that — and thereby introduced a new element into the Space

of Love. This is what my forebears — my forefathers and foremothers — have been doing from time immemorial. Now,
tomorrow will be a special day, and you will see what happens.
Tomorrow will be an important day for the future."

CHAPTER FIFTEEN

A bird for discovering one's soul

The next day we went to the glade and, as before, watched from a concealed vantage-point as our little son was engrossed in his play. The wolf lay at the edge of the glade, following everything with a keen eye. Her cubs played by her side. I noticed little Vladimir from time to time sticking his finger in his mouth and sucking on it, as all children that age do, for some reason. I knew parents are supposed to dissuade their offspring from this habit by some means or other — either by binding the child's hands with cloth or by giving him a soother. I mentioned this to Anastasia, and she replied:

"Not to worry, this is extremely beneficial. Our son is licking pollen from his fingers."

"Pollen? What kind of pollen?"

"Pollen from the flowers and the grass. He touches the flowers and grass with his hands. Sometimes bugs will crawl across his hand, and they carry pollen too, on their legs. See, he is frowning. And taking his finger out of his mouth. That means he did not like the taste of some kind of grass pollen. Now he is bending down and trying to put a flower into his mouth to see how *it* tastes. Let him do that. Let him taste the Universe."

"The Universe and a little flower — what's the connection? Or is it simply a figure of speech?"

"Everything alive in the world has a connection with the Universe."

"But how? Where? Where can one see this connection? What instrument is capable of measuring it?"

"One does not need an instrument. One needs only one's soul. Then you will be able to see and understand what is visible around us every day, many times over."

"What can be seen — and then understood — with the soul? Give me an example."

"Take the Sun, for instance. It is far away from us — a planet of the Universe — yet as soon as it rises, it touches a flower with its ray, and the flower opens in delight. It seems as though they are so far apart from each other — the great huge orb of day and the tiny wee flower, but they are linked together. One cannot exist without the other."

Anastasia unexpectedly fell silent and began looking up. I looked up too. I saw a large eagle circling over the glade. I had seen eagles something like that at the zoo. It kept circling lower and lower, and all at once it touched down with its talons about two metres from the boy. The inertia of its flight kept it moving along the ground for a while. Then, after shaking its feathers all over, it stood forth proud in the glade.

The wolf pricked up her ears. Her fur was standing on end, but she made no move to attack the eagle, which was now strutting proudly across the glade.

The little one got all excited. He sat down on his little bare bottom and — without any awareness of danger — stretched out his hands toward the fearsome bird.

Strutting slowly on its talons, the eagle came right up close to the boy. Its hooked beak hung right over his little head.

The boy apparently felt himself in no danger whatsoever. He began to feel the eagle's feathers and touched its talon-tipped legs. He clapped his little hand against the eagle's chest and smiled.

All at once its huge beak touched the boy's head — then a second time, as if looking for something on it. Then the eagle went off to one side and spread its wings. With a beat of its wings it rose slightly off the ground, and again touched down and stood still. The boy stretched out his arms in the direction of the huge, threatening bird and began uttering sounds: *eh, e-e-eh.*

And all at once the eagle... The eagle went behind the boy's back, and all of a sudden started running, and then it took flight! It circled low over the glade, dived down and without landing picked up the boy in its enormous talons.

But the talons did not pierce his flesh.

The eagle thrust its sharp claws under the boy's armpits and began circling low over the glade, beating its wings and trying to lift the little one off the ground.

The boy jerked his trailing feet along the grass, sometimes ever so slightly lifting them into the air. The boy's eyes were bulging, sparkling with the fire of excitement. And then, all at once, they rose into the air! They had risen a metre above the ground when they achieved synchronicity — when the push of the little feet against the ground coincided with the beat of the eagle's wings.

The eagle kept circling, lifting the two of them gradually higher, but the boy didn't cry out. They simply flew, rising together into the deep blue. By this time the eagle had lifted the boy above the tops of the tall cedars and was continuing to climb.

Overcome with shock, and still speechless, I seized Anastasia's arm. Her eyes remained fixed on the sky as she whispered to herself:

"You are still the strong one! Bravo! And you may indeed be old, but you are still strong. Your wings are still mighty. Fly! Fly even higher!"

And the eagle, bearing in its talons the wee child's little body, kept circling and climbing higher and higher into the heavenly blue.

"What's the point of subjecting the child to an execution like this? Why expose him to such danger?" I yelled at Anastasia, as soon as I had recovered from shock.

"Please do not worry, Vladimir. The eagle's ascent is not nearly as dangerous as the aeroplanes on which you yourself have flown."

"But what if he drops the boy from way up there?"

"He would never even think of such a thing! You just relax, do not allow either fear or doubt into your thoughts. The eagle's flight is making an extremely significant contribution to our son's conscious awareness. Note that the eagle has lifted the child above our Earth."

"What significance can there be here," I countered, "except for superstition? It is quite true that Man should not interfere in great works of creation. With that I agree. But an ascent like this was not provided for by the Creator. You yourself, along with your grandfather, taught the bird to do this. Out of some kind of superstition, most likely. What else could it be? There's no point in taking such a risk!"

"When I was little," came Anastasia's reply, "I too flew up high with this same eagle. I did not have a great deal of understanding back then, but it was so interesting, so extraordinary. The glade seemed so small from up high. And the Earth seemed so broad and unfathomable. Everything was so bright, and this extraordinary experience stayed with me for a long time, for ever. When I had grown some — by this time I was three years old — Great-Grandfather asked me a question:

"'Tell me, Anastasia, do all the creatures like it when you stroke and caress them with your hand?'

"'Yes, they all do. They keep wagging their tails to show how much they like my caressing. The grass and the flowers and the trees like it too, but not all of them have tails to wag, to show how good it feels to be stroked.'

"'So, everything desires to feel the embrace of your hand?'

"'Yes, everything living and growing, small or large.'

"'And the wide Earth also wants to be caressed? You have seen the Earth, how wide it is?'

"At this point I recalled the vivid experience I had had with the eagle as a baby. The size of the Earth was not something I knew just from hearsay. And so I answered Great-Grandfather without hesitating:

"'The Earth is wide, you cannot see its edge. But if everyone wants to be caressed, that means the Earth must want it, too. But who would be able to embrace the whole Earth? It is so great that even *your* arms, Great-Grandfather, would not be able to embrace the whole of the Earth!'

"Great-Grandfather stretched out his arms to either side, looked at them, and nodded in agreement.

"'You are right. Even my arms are not long enough to embrace the whole Earth. But you said that the Earth, like everyone else, wishes to be caressed?'

"'Yes, it does. Everybody wants to be caressed by Man.'

"'So you, Anastasia, should embrace the whole Earth as well. Think about how you could do this,' Great-Grandfather said, and walked away.

"I began thinking a lot of the time about how to embrace the whole Earth. And I could not think of anything. And I knew that Great-Grandfather would not speak to me — he would not ask me any more questions — until I had solved this problem, and so I kept trying.

"More than a month passed, and the problem had not been solved. And then one day I found myself looking tenderly at the wolf, from a distance. She was standing on the other side of the glade.

"All at once, sensing my gaze, the wolf started wagging her tail. Then I began to notice how all the creatures were so delighted when I looked at them with joy and tenderness. How big they were or how far away they were was not important. They were delighted just from my looking at them or thinking about them with love. I realised they were just as happy as they had been earlier when I was stroking them with my hand.

hen I became aware of something: Here was 'I' with my
.ds and feet, and yet there was also this other me, larger
than could be shown by someone's hands. And this larger, invisible entity was also *me*. That meant that every Man was
set up just like me. And this larger me was indeed capable of
embracing the whole Earth.

"When Great-Grandfather showed up, I was all bubbling
with joy, and I said to him:

"'Look, Grandpakins, see how happy all the creatures
are — not just when I touch them with my hand, but also
when I look upon them from a distance. It is invisible, but
something of me is embracing them, and it can embrace the
whole Earth too.

"'I shall embrace the Earth with my invisible self! I am
Anastasia. There is the little me, and there is the greater me.
But how this other me is called, I do not yet know. But I shall
think about how to call it properly, and I shall say its name
and give you the whole answer, Grandpakins! Then will you
begin talking with me again?'

"Great-Grandfather began talking with me right away, and
said:

"'Call your second self, dear granddaughter, *soul. Your* soul.
And cherish it, and act in accord with this limitless soul of
yours.'

"Tell me, Vladimir," Anastasia said, addressing me, "how
old were *you* when you first became aware of your soul, when
you felt it for the first time?"

"I don't remember exactly," I replied, and wondered
whether I had ever really discovered my soul, or whether
others discovered it too, and at what age? And to what
degree? Maybe we simply talk about our soul, not really
feeling at one with it, not really thinking about our second,
invisible self. And how important is it to feel all that, and
what for?

The tiny dot moving overhead quickly began enlarging. The eagle kept circling lower and lower over the glade. When it reached the height of the tree-tops, I could see the little one's flushed face, and his eyes sparkling with excitement. The little fingers at the tips of his outstretched arms were moving in time with the wingbeats of the extraordinary bird. When the little one's legs touched the ground and started trailing across the grass, the eagle loosened its talons. The little one fell, rolled over in the grass and quickly got up on all fours. Then he sat up and started turning his head around, looking for his new-found friend.

The eagle staggered off a little ways, but then fell on its side. It lay awkwardly on the grass about ten metres distant, with one wing sticking out at an angle. It was having a hard time breathing, and its head was resting on the ground.

The little one saw it, broke into a smile and crawled over to it. The eagle attempted to get up and greet the boy, but once again rolled over on its side. Maliciously baring her teeth, the wolf took two leaps and landed between the eagle and the boy. Anastasia whispered, her voice trembling:

"How perfect and strict are Your laws. You gave everything to Man right from the beginning, Creator. The wolf is following your laws, but I feel sorry, very sorry for the eagle."

"What is going on? Why is the wolf acting so aggressive and malicious?" I asked Anastasia.

"Now the wolf will not let the eagle come to Vladimir," she replied. "She thinks it has fallen ill, since it has rolled over on its side. She could attack it to chase it out of the glade. Vladimir must not see the attack — he will not understand it at the present time. Oh, what to do? What can we possibly do?"

At this point the eagle shook its feathers, got up firmly on its feet, proudly threw back its head, and clicked its fearsome beak twice. With proud and sure step the eagle began strutting toward the boy. The wolf appeared to calm down, went off to one side, but not far. She was ready at any moment to make her leap, and followed the proceedings like a hawk.

The little one first touched the enormous bird's beak, then began tugging on its wing feathers, ruffling them and demanding or asking something, repeating all the while: *e-eh, a-ah.*

The bird's hooked beak touched the crown of the boy's head, along with his shoulders, which still bore the marks of the eagle's talons.

Then the eagle bent its head to the ground and, using its beak to tear off a little flower, put it in the boy's open mouth, as though it were feeding its young. The little one all the while kept making the same vowel sounds. After performing this 'parental duty' the eagle began staggering again. The malicious wolf crouched for a leap. And then suddenly the eagle... it started into a run. There was a beating of wings and... take-off!

Time after time it would rise higher and higher, then make a sudden dive for the glade. About a metre and a half from the ground it would level out and ascend once more. The little one waved at it, stretched his arms out to it, called it, laughing with a toothless grin. Anastasia kept her eyes fixed on the eagle, and whispered with concern:

"You do not have to do that. You did everything just right. And you are healthy — I know you are not sick. Relax, my dear eagle, relax. Thank you! I believe... I believe you are well! You are just a little old! Relax!"

Once again the eagle executed its complex pirouette, in such a way as to touch the grass with its talons. Still, it did not land, or push off from the ground. Instead, with a powerful thrust of its wings, it managed to rise in the air, snatching a clump of grass along the way. It circled, showered the little one with the grass and began rising higher and higher into the sky.

As before, Anastasia followed the eagle like a hawk — not taking her eyes away even when it became nothing but a dot in the blue. For some reason I found myself following it too, as the dot grew ever more distant from the glade. At first it went straight up, and then veered sharply off to the side, away from the glade. Suddenly the dot headed for the ground, and it wasn't long before we could see that first one wing and then the other were spreading themselves — but simply from the wind, and not as a deliberate action by the bird.

It was not flapping its wings or soaring — it was simply falling. Its wings were ruffling in the wind — it was the wind that had opened them.

Anastasia exclaimed:

"You died in the sky, way up high! And there you remain. You did all that you could possibly do for Man. Thank you. Thank you for showing us your heights, my old teacher."

The eagle continued to fall, while two young eagles circled overhead.

"Those are your offspring, they are strong already. You did everything for their future too," whispered Anastasia to the old eagle, which had fallen somewhere beyond the glade. As though in death it could still hear her.

By this time the two young eagles were circling low over the glade. I knew they were its offspring, and the little one waved to them.

"Of all things!" I exclaimed to Anastasia. "Why this senseless sacrifice? What did he do that for? And do it all for Man? Why do they try like that, Anastasia? Why do they sacrifice themselves like that?"

"For the light emanating from Man. For the grace which Man can give them, and for a feeling of hope for their offspring. Now *its* offspring will see and sense the light of life-giving love from Man! Look, Vladimir, our son smiled at the young eagles and now they are flying over to him. Perhaps the old eagle has realised that this light, this grace-filled light emanating from Man, will also include a particle of itself."

"Are they ready to sacrifice themselves for the light emanating from *everyone?*"

"From everyone who is capable of emitting this grace-filled light!!!"

CHAPTER SIXTEEN

The system

Anastasia went off to get ready to feed our son, while I once again set out for a walk in the woods to do some thinking.

Two things were bothering me — unpleasant things. The first was how I, as a father, was still unable to find myself a niche where I could participate in the raising of my son. It had become clear to me that I could not come up with any more interesting toys than those he had already. And there was no point in bringing food in either.

Our son already has his mother's milk and fresh flower pollen, and then there will be nuts and berries. Naturally, packaged baby food is no substitute for a living, growing source of nourishment. Yet still I had a hard time mentally accepting this kind of situation.

After all, Anastasia has nothing, and yet at the same time she lacks nothing, and can even make liberal provision for the baby.

In the TV adverts there is such a hype about toys and other stuff for children that it almost seems a child won't survive without them. Here, however, they make no sense at all — more than that, they are actually harmful. A baby doesn't even need a crib here. With a crib like the one he has — namely the bear — of course, he is not going to freeze even when the temperature is minus forty. There's no need to wash sheets or diapers. The bear — can you believe it? — is also a stickler for cleanness. Each time she scrapes clean her groin-area with her claws, just like a comb. She rubs her tummy on the grass, and then bathes. When she comes out of the water she shakes herself off, with spray flying in all directions, then lies down on her back with her tummy up and dries herself off, and then once again combs her groin area.

Anastasia took me over to her and had me feel the place where our little one sleeps. It is soft there, clean and warm.

But even if I am not required to make any kind of material provision, a father should still take part in raising his son — that's for certain. Only how? Maybe I should go to Anastasia and firmly demand a definitive answer. After all, I have fulfilled all her conditions — I have not picked up the baby, nor have I insisted on him making use of the presents I brought with me.

My other disappointment was in not being able to fulfil my readers' requests and lay out a specific system or timetable for raising children. There are a lot of questions in the letters about children, and they are always asked at readers' conferences. I promised that I would definitely question Anastasia about this, and in my next book I would set forth the system her family has used from generation to generation to bring up their young.

And there you have it! Not only does she reject systems in general, but she even declares *any* system to be harmful. Of course, that cannot be. Amidst all the harmful systems there has to be at least one that is right. And then it dawned on me. In all the readers' letters there was not a single question about child-raising addressed to me. Everyone was looking to Anastasia for an answer, and if people actually trust her more than the usual experts in our world — certainly more than they trust me — then it's up to her to answer the questions raised. She's the one who is obliged to do that. My part is simply to lay it out on paper. I've got enough on my plate just putting out the books.

Anastasia finished her tasks and came running over in all her rosy-cheeked cheerfulness.

"Everything is done. Our son is asleep. You have not been too bored here all by yourself?"

"I've been thinking."

"About what?"

"About how there was nothing more to write in my next book. I told you how people are waiting for answers to their specific questions. People are interested in child-raising. But what can I write about that? Sure, I'll tell about how you communicate with the baby, how he's getting on. But what's the point? In the conditions of our world that kind of régime is simply not practicable. Nobody's going to train a bear or a wolf or an eagle, and nobody has a glade with pure pollen on the flowers as you have here."

"But it is not the bear that is important, Vladimir! Nor the eagle. They are merely effects. There is just one thing that is important, and it will find the right path under any conditions."

"And what's that?"

"One's attitude to one's child. The thoughts surrounding the child. Believe me, and try to understand. Christ could be born only by a mother who believed that Christ would be born to her, and if the parents have the same attitude to their child as they would to Christ or Mohammed, their offspring will follow this thought. And he will become whoever he aspires to become. People will still explore Nature, and those who are able to feel and become aware of what the Creator has created — its sense and purpose — they will be able to make a bright and happy world for their child."

"But how do they feel this? There has to be, somehow, a gradual process. There has to be a procedure."

"This can be felt only with the heart. Only the heart is capable of understanding it."

"And more specifically?"

"You wrote 'more specifically' when you told about the dachniks,[1] yet you took no notice yourself. What is the point of wasting more words? If the heart and the soul are not open, the words will simply vanish with the wind, barely noticeable."

"Yes, I did write a few words about that. But nothing has come of them in real life."

"Young shoots are barely noticeable, they are not seen by everyone right off. All the more so in the case of young shoots growing in the soul."

"But if you can't see them, what's the point in writing? I write, I try, but still there are many who do not believe or understand what you are talking about. And there are some who even doubt your existence."

"Think about it, Vladimir — perhaps you will be able to see some logic even in their doubts."

"What kind of logic can there be in their doubts?"

"Doubts make counter-actions less likely, and that is why I exist for those for whom I exist. They and I co-exist together side by side, in each other's hearts. If you think about it a bit longer, it will make sense to you. I exist because of them. They have the power to engender, to create and not to destroy. They will understand you and support you, and will be mentally by your side."

"You can say what you like, but I am tired of listening to insulting remarks. Dispel the doubts of the unbelievers. Come and show yourself on television, show something of your extraordinary abilities," I implored Anastasia, and she replied:

"Believe me, Vladimir, my appearance in the flesh and any miracles performed in public will not pour the light of faith into the faithless. They will only exacerbate the feeling of irritation on the part of those who do not like someone else's perception of the world. And you should not waste your

---

[1]*dachniks* — people who spend time (their days off, especially summer holidays) tending a garden at their *dacha,* or cottage in the country. See further details in Book 1.

energies on them. To everything there is a season, to every-thing there is a dawn, and if you wish, I *shall* come forth to people and I shall appear in the flesh. But before that I must make it so women who have involuntarily consecrated their lives to the kitchen can experience joys of a different order. And so that the light of love may shine upon young mothers who have been left alone with their children. And *the children*! You see, *the children*! Their souls must be liberated from the tyranny of theories."

"See, there you go again with your dream. A lot of time has gone by since you started to dream that way, but little has actually been done. We've got a book, there's pictures and poetry, but where are your global achievements for all peo-ple? Only don't talk of bright little shoots growing in peo-ple's souls. Show something tangible, something that can be felt in real life... You can't show anything, can you?"

"I can."

"Then show it!"

"If I show it, I shall be subjecting you to the temptation to open prematurely the little shoots which are just starting to come up, and then who will protect them from a damaging hailstorm?"

"*You* will."

"In that case I shall be obliged to do so, to correct my mis-take. Look..."

At that point, thanks to Anastasia, I was able to witness a phenomenon which was even more extraordinary and over-whelming than anything I had described in my books to date. Within the space of a single moment — either inside me or in front of me, I'm not sure which — there paraded a multitude of marvellous faces of people of different ages and from dif-ferent parts of the Earth.

This was not just any series of flickering images. Not just people's faces, but their splendid actions too appeared before my eyes. I could see the circumstances surrounding them — the events that were happening to them or because of them over their whole lifetime. They were all drawn from our present reality. It would have taken many years to view such a quantity of information on a cinema screen, yet here it took but a single moment, after which Anastasia was standing once more before me, in exactly the same position she was in before. She began speaking the moment I saw her:

"You were thinking, Vladimir, that what you saw was merely a kind of hypnosis. I ask you please not to try to guess the means by which these people appeared before you. We were talking about children. About the most important thing! Did you see the children? Tell me."

"Yes, I saw the children. Their faces looked intelligent and kind. The children were building a house all by themselves, a very beautiful house, and so big. And they were singing while they worked. And I saw a grey-haired man amongst them. This man was a scholar, an academician. And he appeared to me right off to be very wise. Only he was talking in a peculiar fashion. He seemed to think that children could be wiser even than those whom we call professors. The children were talking with this academician as an equal, and yet at the same time with respect. Indeed, there was a lot about children in my vision. About how different their education was, the things they dreamt about. But that's *only* a vision, so what's the point in carrying on about it? In real life things are not like that at all."

"What you saw was indeed real life, Vladimir, and before long you will be persuaded of that yourself."

And, to my amazement, it all came about, just as Anastasia promised. It happened! And I saw it!

CHAPTER SEVENTEEN

Put your vision of happiness into practice

Soon after returning from the taiga I went once again to the city of Gelendzhik[1] to attend a reader's conference on the *Anastasia* book. The Governor's aide in charge of the Gelendzhik district of the Krasnodar region took me to see Academician Mikhail Petrovich Shchetinin's[2] forest school.

A narrow gravel road led from the main highway into the forest, to a valley nestled amidst the mountain peaks. The road soon came to an end in front of a most unusual two-storey mansion. It was still under construction. From one of the still frameless window openings wafted the sounds of children's voices singing a Russian folk song. This building was part of the vision Anastasia had showed me back in the taiga forest, but now it was an altogether real experience.

Without a word to anyone I made my way through various construction materials to touch this mansion with my own hands. As I approached, I saw a little girl, about ten years old, climbing deftly down a ladder. She went over to a pile of river

[1]The author's earlier experiences at Gelendzhik are described in Book 1, Chapter 30: "Author's message to readers" and Book 2, Chapter 33: "Your sacred sites, O Russia!". Gelendzhik is located in the Krasnodar region of the northern Caucasus, on the north-east shore of the Black Sea.

[2]*Mikhail Petrovich Shchetinin* (1944–) — director (principal) of the Tekos School near Gelendzhik. Originally a music teacher by profession, Mikhail Petrovich has had a long and distinguished career in experimental education. The recipient of several awards, in 1991 he was honoured with the title *Akademik* (Academician) by the Russian Academy of Education.

pebbles and began selecting and dropping stones into an old herring tin. When she started back up the ladder, I climbed up after her, in the direction of the alluring music pouring forth from above.

There on the second floor I watched as a group of kids like her, some a little older, were taking smooth pebbles out of a box and attaching them with a cement mixture to the wall, making an amazingly beautiful pattern. Two little girls at once carefully washed off each newly attached stone with damp rags. They set about their tasks in earnest, singing as they worked. No adults were present. Later I found out that the whole foundation, indeed, each brick of this structure, had been laid by a child's hand. The children had come up with the whole design by themselves, including every corner of their building.

And this is not the only such building on the little campus. In this amazing setting children are constructing not only their buildings, their campus, but their whole future in the process. And they *sing!* Here a ten-year-old girl is capable of building a house, doing splendid drawings and cooking meals, not to mention knowing ballroom dance steps and mastering the fundamentals of Russian martial arts.[3]

The children of this forest school are acquainted with Anastasia. They themselves told me about her. Three hundred pupils from different Russian cities study here.

At this school children take but a year to master the whole ten-year public-school maths syllabus, along with studying three foreign languages. They neither recruit nor produce child prodigies. They simply give the kids a chance to discover what already lies within.

Academician Mikhail Petrovich Shchetinin's school comes under the Russian Federation's Ministry of Education. It

---

[3]Photos of the campus, pupils and creative learning activities may be found on the colour insert of the present volume.

charges no tuition fees. Even though the school does not advertise itself, it has no vacancies. Indeed, there is already a waiting list of 2,500 hopefuls for an unexpected opening.

It is hard to find words to describe the joy on these children's beaming faces. I went to visit the school directly after the readers' conference at Gelendzhik. I went with a small group of readers who had heard about my intended visit.

One of these readers was Natalia Sergeevna Bondarchuk,[4] an actress and film director who is also on the board of the Roerich Society.[5] A specialist in esoterics, she gave a presentation at the conference on the Roerichs' legacy and on esoterics in general. She talked about Anastasia far more intelligently than I.

Natalia Sergeevna was accompanied by her ten-year-old daughter Mashenka.[6] After the conference the two of them were to go to a film festival in Anapa,[7] where Mashenka's beloved grandmother, the famous actress Inna Makarova,[8] was

---

[4]*Natalia Sergeevna Bondarchuk* (1950–) — a popular Russian film actress and director. One of her first cinema roles was in Tarkovsky's famous 1973 sci-fi flick *Solaris*. She has directed a number of children's films, including several on the *Bambi* theme.

[5]*the Roerich Society* — founded by Russian expert on Oriental religions Elena Ivanovna Roerich [Rerikh] and her artist-husband Nikolai Konstantinovich Roerich (see footnote 18 in Book 1, Chapter 1: "The ringing cedar"). With branches in a number of countries, the society is devoted to the study and promotion of art and culture in relation to human creativity and spirituality. It sees Culture as a synthesis of ethics, religion, science and art, all contributing to Man's spiritual development.

[6]*Mashenka* — a diminutive form of the name *Maria*.

[7]*Anapa* — a Black Sea coastal resort with a population of approximately 60,000, located about 100 km north-west of Gelendzhik.

[8]*Inna Makarova* (1926–) — an award-winning Russian film star who made her début in 1948 with *Molodaya gvardia* (Young Guard). In 1984 she appeared in a film version of Gogol's classic novel *Mertvye dushi* (Dead Souls). She has also starred in several Bondarchuk films. In 2001 she received official congratulations from President Putin on her 75th birthday.

already staying. But Mashenka's words came as a thunderous call to new enlightenment:

"Mamochka, please, just for three days. Just three! While you go to the festival, arrange for me to stay here at this school!"

And the delicate little Mashenka stayed for three days at the school, to the great astonishment of her mother, who sadly said:

"Apparently we don't give enough to our children — even though we love them, we are inadvertently stealing from them."

Natalia Sergeevna was accompanied by a film cameraman. He began shooting as soon as the children of Shchetinin's school started talking about their communication with Anastasia and their understanding of life. I'd like to reproduce here some of our conversation with the children who were building this mansion. Natalia Sergeevna and I were the ones asking the questions:

"One gets the impression that each brick of your building here is filled with the bright energy of a great power."

"Yes, that's true," answered an older, red-haired girl. "So much depends on the people who touch them. We have done all this with love, we are trying with our mental attitude to bring only what is good and happy to our future."

"Who designed this building, the columns and paintings?"

"This was the result of our united, collective thinking."

"Does that mean that while each one is outwardly working on their own individual task, in actual fact it represents a collective thought?"

"That's right. Every evening we get together and plan out, or visualise, the day ahead. We come up with the images we want to see expressed in the design of our mansion. Some of the pupils here take on the role of architect — they give specific form to our common work, tie it all together."

"What image is expressed in the room we're standing in now?"

"The image of Svarog[9] — the primordial element of heavenly fire. You can see him here in the symbols, in the pebble amulets."

"Does your group recognise one of its own as a principal or superior?"

"We do have a leader, but by and large it is the collective thought that is at work here — *lava,* we call it.

"Say that again — thought is *lava?*"

"That's right — a state of mind, an image, a desire."

"Do you all work with such great delight, everybody smiling, everybody with such sparkling eyes — everybody so cheerful?"

"Yes, our life is like that, since we are doing what we want, doing what we can, doing what we love to do."

"You said each stone has its own pulse and rhythm?"

"Yes, and this pulse beats once a day — just once."

"Is it like that with all stones, or do some beat twice a day?"

"Every stone's pulse beats once a day."

"Doesn't it seem to you that your mansion is something like a temple?"

"A temple is not a form, but a state of mind. For example, the cupolas — they simply help you access a particular state of mind. The form is moulded by feeling. And it is not

---

[9]*Svarog* — in Russian and Slavic mythology, the god of fire, the father and divine light of celestial and earthly fires, who created (Russian: *svarganil*) our Universe (Sanskrit and ancient Russian: *svarga*). Svarog fought and captured a giant malicious serpent or dragon (*Zmey*), which he used to pull a plough, separating the land of the living (or the visible world, *Yav*) from the land of the dead (or the invisible world, *Nav*) and thus establish order (or Rightness, *Prav*). In Christianity he is associated with, among others, the Archangel Michael.

by chance that the form of a cupola or hipped roof[10] came to us — they represent our aspirations for heaven and the descent of Heavenly Grace."

"This building, where every stone is laid with a good thought, is it able to heal?"

"Of course."

"And *does* it heal?"

"Yes, it does."

I couldn't help looking at the girls attaching the river-pebble ornamental design to the walls of the upper room. The girls were dressed in very plain, unsophisticated attire, they were beautiful, only with an unusual kind of beauty. I thought to myself: where do we go to meet our future wives? To dance-halls, parties and resorts, eh? We see our future wives all made up wearing the latest fashions, luring us with their slender legs and other charms of their figure. All this is what we marry, and then later, when the make-up is rubbed off, you look, and there you see sitting before you a *kikimora,*[11] and looking like a *kikimora,* grumbling away and demanding attention and... love. What happiness is there in living your whole life with a *kikimora* — what is there to talk about with her? And then she demands you support her financially too. Oh, what rotten luck! But just maybe we get what we deserve. Of course we get what we deserve. You have to be a complete idiot to marry make-up and long legs! But some of us

---

[10]*hipped roof* — a pyramid-style roof with 4 or more sloping sides, narrower at the top than at the bottom — characteristic of many Russian churches of wooden or stone construction.

[11]*kikimora* — in Slavic mythology and folk customs, a malevolent female ghost said to attach itself to a particular house and disturb the inhabitants, males in particular. By extension, the term may also suggest an ugly woman in shabby clothing, ill-tempered and grumbling, striving to make life of her husband (and men in general) unbearable.

are lucky. Some of us end up marrying, well... these girls here, the ones sticking the ornamental stones on the walls. They will be able to build a beautiful house, and to cook meals with love, they know all sorts of foreign languages, they're wise, smart, beautiful, and when they grow up they'll become still more beautiful, even without cosmetics. Naturally, many will want to take them to wife, but who will they agree to marry? This was a question we put to these beautiful little girls wearing their plain clothing:

"Tell me, who would you like to marry, what kind of husband would you like? What qualities should he have?"

And right away, without hesitation, the first girl responded:

"Kindness, patience... and he should be a Man who loves his Motherland. A Man with honour and dignity."

"And what is honour, in your view?"

"For me, honour can be summed up in one saying: I have the honour of being Russian."

"And what constitutes a Russian Man?"

"It is a Man who loves his Motherland. First and foremost it is one who stands up for her and never fails her. Not for a moment, not even the most difficult moment. He feels himself a part of *Rus.*"[12]

"And your children will live for the Motherland?"

"Yes!"

"And that means your husband must share this view as well?"

"Yes!"

The second girl answered the question as follows:

---

[12] *Rus* (pronounced *ROOS,* rhyming with *moose*) — the name of the Old Russian territory, which by the 9th century A.D. was centred around Kiev; more so than the later term *Rossiya,* it signifies an emotional attachment to the Russian Motherland.

"He should be a Man capable of giving light and warmth to other people. If he radiates light and warmth, it will be good for those around him, and our family too. A Man rich in spirit, healthy in spirit, and this can't be compared with any other kind of riches."

The littlest girl wasn't asked any questions while the camera was running, but later I put the same query to her and got the following response:

"Maybe all the best men will get married while I am growing up, but my husband will still be very good, kind and happy — I shall make him that way, I shall help him the way Anastasia does."

And I saw, and realised that Anastasia was sharing her abilities with these children. Why with the children of Shchetinin's school? Because Academician Mikhail Petrovich Shchetinin is himself a great magician — one who has created and continues to create a big Space of Love, and it will continue to grow even bigger.

Right now these girls are little Anastasias with their light-brown braids. But they will grow up! They will spread across the Earth, creating oases like this one, until the whole Earth is filled with them.

As I was standing there in the upper room on the second storey of this extraordinary mansion, examining the ornamental design and drawings executed by the children's hands (though more reminiscent of the art of the 'old masters'), I had the impression of being in the greatest, brightest and most welcoming temple on Earth. This was probably because the amount of bright energy in this mansion, every millimetre of which had been lovingly caressed by children's hands, was infinitely greater than in many religious temples.

And then I had another thought come to me. Here we'll continue to go about restoring ruined churches and monasteries using modern technology and reinforced concrete construction — not such a difficult thing to do, really — and then we'll come to these temples with the feeling that we have done our duty and begin asking: "Lord, bless our work!" But no blessings will be received. Because during this time God will be concentrating His attention on the children constructing this extraordinary temple building. And He will be concerned that they will run out of cement and not have enough bricks and boards for the floor. And God will lovingly bless all those who help them.

And I couldn't resist the temptation to show the world these little 'shoots'. I couldn't resist doing what Anastasia was so afraid of. And this is how it happened:

I was walking down the aisle between rows of kitchen tables set up outdoors for the children to work at, when I suddenly felt a soft warmth in my body, as though someone was training a heat-reflector on me. The sensation of warmth was similar to that emitted by Anastasia when she concentrated her gaze on a person. Only this time it was considerably weaker. In any case I stopped and looked in the direction the warmth appeared to be coming from. An eleven-year-old girl winnowing rice at a distant table was looking at me and smiling. I went over and sat down beside her. Up close I could see her eyes sparkling with a fiery blue light and I began to feel an even greater sensation of warmth. I asked her her name.

"Hello!" she replied. "My name is Nastia."[13]

"So, you have the ability to warm someone with your gaze, like Anastasia?"

"Did you feel it?"

"Yes, I did."

Little Nastia indeed had Anastasia's ability to warm a person's body with her gaze, although not to the same extent.

[13]*Nastia* — a diminutive form of the name *Anastasia* (a common girl's name in modern Russian).

Natalia Sergeevna, the actress, came and sat down with us, and the cameraman began shooting. With no trace of embarrassment and without interrupting her work, Nastia started answering our questions.

"Where do you get your knowledge and abilities from?"

"From the stars."

"What have you learnt through your communication with Anastasia in Siberia?"

"I've learnt how very important it is to understand and love our Motherland."

"Why is it so important?"

"Because our Motherland is what has been created by our forebears — both distant and close."

"Who are your parents? Where does your father work?"

"My Papa is a schoolteacher. It's nice in the school where he works too, but here it's better."

"Here you are all living as a single friendly, happy family. Have you forgotten about your parents?"

"On the contrary. We love our parents more and more, we send them good thoughts so they can live well, too."

The camera was running, and I very much wanted Nastia to show the sceptics her warming gaze. And so I asked her:

"Nastia, now you can show *many* people how to warm someone with your gaze. See the camera? Look straight into the lens and share your warmth with everyone who will see this."

"To warm everybody at once — that's really hard. I might not be able to do it."

But I kept insisting. I repeated my request. And exactly the same thing started happening with Nastia as happened with Anastasia back in the forest, when she tried to save with her ray at a distance a man and a woman from being tortured by bandits. I described this scene in my first book.[14]

---

[14]See Book 1, Chapter 28: "Strong people".

Back then Anastasia had initially expressed reservations:

"It is not within my power," she had said. "Everything has been, so to speak, programmed in advance, but not by me. I cannot interfere directly. They have the upper hand right now."

And yet, after my repeated requests, she did what I asked her to. She did it, knowing full well that she might die in the process.

And now, after my persistent pleading, little Nastia attempted to do my bidding. Twice in a row, without exhaling, she inhaled air, closed her eyes for a few moments and then began to calmly look straight into the camera lens. The astonished cameraman fell silent. And then all of a sudden Natalia Sergeevna tore off her kerchief and put it over Nastia's head. She was the first to notice how her body had begun to vibrate and her face had turned pale.

I realised I should not have persisted with my request — there was no point in wasting energy on unbelievers. It would only intensify their anger and resistance.

The grown-up visitors could not resist the impulse to touch the children. They touched them, hugged them and patted them as though they were kittens. And why had I brought along a whole group of these grown-ups? After all, I was aware that this school receives visits from all sorts of committees and delegations, and even individuals come to have a look and satisfy their curiosity, and tune into the grace emanating from its inhabitants. And they do come and tune in, and take away, but do not make any contribution of their own.

Perhaps Anastasia was right when she said:

"In trying to gain the grace of a holy place, think what you might offer in return. And if you have not learnt to emit light yourself, then why take it and bury it in yourself, as though in a grave?"

I too had come to the school more out of curiosity than anything else. It was thanks to Anastasia that I had been so graciously received by Academician Shchetinin, and the children had prepared a feast for me and my whole entourage. And it was far more than food that we took away from the table. The sparkle in the children's bright eyes gave us infinitely more, and what were we to give them in return? A patronising pat on the head? I was so angry with myself that I withdrew from the group and went off on my own to think.

All of a sudden I became aware of the two girls whose acquaintance I had made — Lena and Nastia — standing at my side.

"Just relax," Nastia said quietly. "Grown-ups are always that way. They want to pat our heads and give us a hug. They think hugging is the most important thing. And you've been on pins and needles the whole day. Come along with us to our glade, and we'll tell you about Anastasia. I know what space she is in right now."

When we arrived at the glade, the cameraman who had joined us proposed:

"Let's get another interview with the girls. We'll get some excellent shots here — look what a splendid landscape there is, and no one's around to bother us."

"Maybe not," I hesitated. "We've probably tired them out already with so much questioning."

"But still they'll be delighted to talk with you. They don't really like visitors and journalists coming around here. We've got a golden opportunity under our noses. It'd be a shame to let it slip by. Please understand my professional interest."

I grabbed the microphone and told the girls:

"We have to do another interview with you. I'll be asking you some questions and you answer them. Is that okay with you?"

"If you need to, go ahead and ask," replied Lena, and Nastia added: "Of course, of course, we'll be happy to answer."

The girls took up a position right beside us and straightened their long brown braids. They looked me straight in the eye, waiting for my first question.

After two rather trite questions I fell silent, suddenly realising that these were the type of hackneyed, stereotyped questions they got from all the grown-up visitors, committee members and journalists, whereas in fact they were capable of answering questions on themes most adults would never even have cross their minds in their whole lifetime. A Cossack hetman was right when he said:

"My son's been studying here only three months, and I already feel there's a lot more I need to become aware of myself and quickly, or I'm going to look positively stupid next to him."

In any case, aren't we talking down to the children with our immature questions, inadvertently implying they're not capable of responding to anything more? I stood silently before these girls, holding the microphone in my hand, and saw in their faces how concerned they were for me. They realised I had lost my train of thought and didn't know what I should talk with them about. I admitted as much to them:

"You know, I really don't know what to talk to you about, or even what questions I should be asking."

And then ensued an utterly comic situation. Here we were, the cameraman and I, two stout grown-up fellows, and there in front of us were these two young girls, enthusiastically giving each other support, without a second's hesitation explaining to us how to do an interview, how to make conversation with another human being.

"Just relax," they insisted. "You've got to learn how to relax. The most important thing is to be sincere and talk about anything you're concerned about.

"Don't think about us. Of course you should think about any other person you're talking with, but you don't need to think about us if you find that too hard. Just relax.

"Just ask your questions from the heart, we'll be able to answer, don't worry about us.

"As long as you're having trouble, let us tell you something ourselves..."

The girls were walking around the meadow, smiling, feeling the blades of grass and talking. The depth of their understanding of the Universe, the purity emanating from their heart, their eyes sparkling with kindness, literally immersed us in a sense of peace and confidence. The cameraman shot from a distance, not bothering to attempt switching camera angles. Later I would spend hours watching and re-watching the videotape Natalia Sergeevna subsequently gave to me. I would be fascinated by these little charmers with their light-brown braids walking through the glade. They will grow up! There are three hundred of them at the school.

I am writing about this school not to prove anything to anyone, but to gladden the hearts of those who have come to feel and understand Anastasia through my books.

If anyone feels irritated by what I write and how I write it, they need not read my books at all. I have already had my fill of criticism — over my writing style, my grammatical mistakes and the suggestion of a commercial ulterior motive. In any case I am still working on my next book. If you don't like my books, don't bother reading the next one. The events it describes are even more penetrating than the ones recorded in the volumes to date, and my style is getting better, but not by very much. Both the contents and the style could make you quite distraught.

CHAPTER EIGHTEEN

Academician Shchetinin

Who is he? We are accustomed to describing a person through his biographical outline, his record of service, the titles bestowed upon him. But in the present instance all that would be meaningless. In the Bible it says: "By their fruits ye shall know them."[1] Academician Shchetinin's fruits are the happy, beaming faces of the children studying at his school, along with those of their parents. Then, who is he?

Natalia Sergeevna Bondarchuk is not only an award-winning Russian actress, she is also a member of the board of the International Roerich Foundation (a UN non-governmental organisation). She told me:

"I have talked with many famous preachers and teachers in various countries of the world, but I have never been so impressed as here. We may well have come into contact with a great Vedun.[2] I say a *Vedun* not because of his acquaintance with the Old Vedic scriptures, but because he knows what many of us don't."

I should also like to record *my* impressions from my meetings with Mikhail Petrovich Shchetinin, but I am not a specialist in the educational field and hence my terminology may not be all that accurate, so I shall try to reproduce his own words as faithfully as possible.

---

[1]Matth. 7: 20 (*Authorised King James Version*).

[2]*Vedun* (pron. *ve-DOON*) — in Slavic and Hindu traditions: a revered wise man. The word is derived from the Old Slavic (originally Indo-European) root *ved-* meaning *knowing* or *knowledge*.

At one point I was walking down a corridor of the school building, along with Natalia Sergeevna, her cameraman and Mikhail Petrovich. We came to a spacious hall opening onto the corridor, where a number of tables had been set up. At these sat children of various ages, all intensely engaged in some kind of mysterious project, from which neither our presence nor that of the videocamera could distract them. From time to time one or another of the children would get up and go off somewhere, and then come back again. Sometimes they would go over to examine numbers on a bulletin-board hanging on the wall, at other times they would thoughtfully pace around the room. Some of them were talking amongst themselves — arguing or explaining things to each other.[3]

"Mikhail Petrovich, what is going on?" asked Natalia Sergeevna.

"Here you are basically witnessing attempts to establish contact. If the contact is successful, the children will be able to master the ten-year school maths programme in just one year. That is their assignment. It will happen when the children are able to make contact with those who possess similar knowledge, and the degree of openness in their relationships is important. Their field elements[4] will then be able to share information with each other.

"You're familiar with the observation made by simple folk: 'love at first sight', when people in love catch each other's meaning with hardly a word between them. You haven't even opened your mouth, and he's already got it. You can see the whole point here is to make the children feel free and

---

[3]A photo of a typical learning session may be found on the colour insert of the present volume.

[4]*field elements* — referring to the non-material elements making up one's identity. For a more detailed discussion of 'field' phenomena see footnote 13 in Book 2, Chapter 1: "Alien or Man?".

unencumbered. This is a place they can ask any question, get up, and come and go as they please. Maintaining relationships is the important thing.

"Working on relationships is not only very important for the children but also for the ones organising the activities. So we take off the brakes, so to speak, we refrain from focusing on age. Over there, right next to fifteen-year-old Ivan Alexandrovich is sitting ten-year-old Masha. We also have a university student named Sergei Alexandrovich, who's actually finishing university this year."

"And how old is he?"

"He'll turn eighteen this year."

"And he's finishing university at seventeen?"

"Seventeen, in this generation, but we generally try not to refer to the notion of age. That's a very important point. If you will notice, here the teachers tend to blend in with the pupils. True, it is a rather special group. The ones you see here are those that weren't able to participate in the construction. And they have quite a task ahead of them — assimilating the ten-year school maths course, so they in turn will be able to share their knowledge with those who are currently occupied in the construction. And it will all come about. Because what is germinating in them is a system of interdependent integration elements.

"Our collective ancestral memory has knowledge of the laws of the Cosmos, as well as techniques for living in cosmic space. So it is very important to reject any suggestion that there is something they don't know. If one of those doing the explaining entertains such a thought, his pupils will *not* know it. The explainer's basic task is to enter into a relationship with his pupils focused on solving problems, then the learning process takes place all by itself. So as not to distract them with attention to the actual learning or memorisation. The thought of somebody out there *teaching* has to be rejected.

As they work together, the consciousness of a dividing line between teacher and pupil is obliterated.

"The problem-solving process brings with it the necessary knowledge, and what actually takes place is a recalling of things forgotten. This is the reflex arc, you know, as in Pavlov:[5] stimulus-reaction. When necessary, I decide.

"It is very important that what they do should have a direct effect on people around them. And now they are studying not for themselves, that is very important. They are concerned about how to share what they are learning with others. Marks aren't important to them. They know that in a few days they will have to explain it all to someone else.

"They have been entrusted with the beginning of the learning process. Each pupil you see here has been assigned a group. He observes how his designated pupils work on the construction and watches to see that members of his group do not fall behind their schoolmates. Considerable emphasis is laid on motivation — the idea of service to others. And if they learn anything, they learn to understand the soul, the aspirations and the thoughts of another individual. It's not the mathematics that's important here, but rather Man learning mathematics. Not maths for its own sake, but maths for the sake of progress toward Truth. And the more powerful this *for the sake of* motive is, the more successful will be one's immersion into a field of knowledge.

"It is important to be in an atmosphere of sincerity, with no feelings of being offended or irritated. *That's wrong* is a phrase we never use. In the Old Russian language there is no stoppage of motion and no bad words. In ancient times people,

---

[5] *Ivan Petrovich Pavlov* (1849–1936) — world-renowned Russian physiologist, recipient of the 1904 Nobel Prize in Medicine for his work on digestion; he later became famous for his experiments with dogs and theories of human behaviour based on conditioned reflexes.

no matter what their ethnic affiliation, never used a bad word in reference to anything. It simply doesn't exist, so why pay attention to it? What is bad does not exist. If you find yourself at a dead-end, then the words you would use to get out of that dead-end would be phrases like: *turn right, turn left, climb up* — hinting at which way one should go, but not snapping: 'You're standing the wrong way.' Today russophobes commit sacrilege by saying 'Speak Russian!', when they actually mean cursing. That is not Russian at all. Kobzev[6] has a very succinct expression of this thought:

> *From our Slav forebears we have heard*
> *Midst happenings of great dimension,*
> *They paid to language, phrase and word*
> *A special homage and attention.*

"That is true. So people who work with them should have a deep vocabulary range which excludes thought-distracting, incidental words. Words warmed by feelings have special significance.

"Truth, their legacy — it's all spiritual. The child must be enrolled in a natural cosmic process — eternal self-reproduction. Then you have given the child eternity, the joy of life, real existence. Not just illusory forms, like: 'See here, son, I've bought you a shirt and trousers and shoes — now I can die.' But what have you really given your son? Your gifts, after all, won't last more than a single season! If only you had given your son your good name, your honour, your work, your

---

[6] *Igor Ivanovich Kobzev* (1924–1986) — a Russian poet known for his verse based on the history of Russia and the ancient Slavs — in particular, on the celebrated poetic chronicle *Slovo o polku Igoreve* (The song of Igor's campaign). In 1977 he helped organise a museum devoted to the famous chronicle. Kobzev himself is best known, perhaps, for his epic tale *Padenie Peruna* (The Fall of Perun).

friends, a flourishing people! If you had given him an under-standing of the Truth of being and a life of wisdom, *then* you could say: 'Son, I have given you the most important thing, you will be happy. You will buy shirts and build houses, you know now how it is done.'"

Listening to Academician Shchetinin speak and observing his interactions with the children, I noticed that they were very much like what Anastasia had said about children, and I wondered: how could a lonely Siberian recluse and this grey-haired academic think so much alike — almost identically, in fact? And, come to think of it, why is he talking with me at all? Why did he receive me so warmly, even setting the table and offering me a meal? He's taken me around the school, shown me everything. Why? What kind of education expert am I? I'm nobody. One who used to get pretty poor marks in school. But of course — Anastasia's somehow been at it again."

Of course it was only thanks to Anastasia that I ended up at Shchetinin's school in the first place. But he and I didn't talk about her. We talked about all sorts of other things — everyday things. Each time I visited we would walk around and see how the construction of this unusual temple building was progressing. As for my book, he said tersely: "It's very ac-curate" — and that was it.

A few days after my first visit — after the day I had come with a group of conference participants, and had shown them Nastia, asking her to warm everybody with her gaze — the following incident occurred. Mikhail Petrovich and I were walking along one of the school corridors, and I was keeping my eye peeled for her. I searched for her the way people in-tuitively search for a source which emits light.

"Nastia's light has gone out," Shchetinin said all of a sud-den. "Right now I'm in the process of restoring her strength. It's coming along, but slowly. She'll need some time to fully recover."

"What do you mean, it's gone out? Why? She's a strong lass. What happened?"

"Yes, she is strong. But she had a very powerful emotional outburst."

I stood there in Shchetinin's office, angry and irritated at myself. Why had I done such a thing? For just whose benefit was I trying to prove something? I had utterly failed to heed Anastasia's warning: "Neither my appearance in the flesh nor any miracles performed in public will pour the light of faith into the faithless. They will only exacerbate the feeling of irritation on the part of those who do not like someone else's perception of the world."[7]

That's enough, I thought to myself. I shall no longer try to show people and I shan't write any more. That's it. Look what a mess I've made with my writing! I was thinking this to myself, but then Shchetinin suddenly said out loud:

"You shouldn't stop writing, Vladimir." Then he came over to me, placed his hand on my shoulder and, looking me straight in the eye, began vocalising a tune. I could hear how easily he took the high notes, but even more amazing was the fact that the melody he was vocalising was very similar to the one Anastasia had sung for me in the taiga.

As I made my way back to the main door, I passed the same hall where the pupils were still scurrying about. There was Nastia, sitting on a chair. I went over to her. She got up, raised her head, and her rather weary-looking eyes brightened in a second, emitting light and warmth with their sparkle. I realised now that she was giving of her energy and warmth to others. She was giving her all, without reservation, to help that other Anastasia, the one in Siberia, fulfil her dream. For it had now become their shared dream.

[7]From Book 3, Chapter 16: "The system".

So what *was* going on here? What was the force behind that dream? Why were they...? With complete self-sacrifice... And the child's gaze... Is it possible to become worthy, even partially worthy, of such a gaze during a single lifetime? I wondered. Aloud I said:

"Well, hello, Nastia!" And to myself: "You don't have to, Nastia. Thank you. Forgive me."

"I'll see you out," the girl offered. "Lena and I will go with you to your car."

As we drove off, I kept looking behind me until the car rounded a corner, watching the little figures standing there at the end of the road, by the mansion, under a lamp-post, as they got smaller and smaller. They weren't waving their arms in the usual sign of farewell. Each of them held one hand raised in the air, palm out-turned in the direction of the departing vehicle. I knew what this meant — Shchetinin had explained it to me earlier. It signified: "We send you our rays of good, may they follow you wherever you go." And once more I felt fired up with the thought: "What do I need to accomplish to become worthy of your rays?"

CHAPTER NINETEEN

What to agree with, what to believe?

My meeting with Mikhail Petrovich Shchetinin and my acquaintance with his amazing school took place after my second visit to Anastasia. After seeing this school I had virtually no lingering doubts about Anastasia's pronouncements on raising children, or about the way she communicated with our son. But back there in the taiga everything within me had rebelled against her. I didn't want to believe her. At least not everything she said.

As I write these lines I can hear many readers saying, either aloud or to themselves: "Come on, how could he possibly doubt? After all, there have been so many times he was obliged to concede that she was right, and still he carries on like an idiot, unable to perceive a new phenomenon!"

My daughter Polina sent me a videocassette from one of the readers' conferences. I watched as a scholar from Novosibirsk by the name of Speransky[1] declared right from the podium:

"Megré is incapable of fully grasping what Anastasia says. He hasn't the brains for it."

I do not feel offended by him — on the contrary, his whole talk was most interesting. The audience listened with bated

---

[1] *Sergei Vladimirovich Speransky* — a biology expert with Novosibirsk Scientific Research Institute, known for his experiments using mice to detect extra-sensory abilities; a Corresponding Member of the International Academy of Energy-Informational Sciences.

breath, and thanks to him I have been able to comprehend that Anastasia is an *Essence* — a self-sufficient substance.

I myself have no expertise in such matters — I've been involved in a completely different line of work. But what about all those who are into studying Nature, or children — why have they been keeping so quiet, barely uttering a peep about what they know? And even children in their letters to me tell me I should be more attentive to what Anastasia says and does.

But I can respectfully assure my readers that I have indeed become much more attentive to her; nevertheless, I cannot refrain from arguing with her, or from doubting. I cannot refrain since I am unwilling to admit that I and our whole society are complete idiots. I am unwilling to believe that we are heading down a path of degeneration.

And so I am trying to find at least some justification for our actions. Or some reason for saying her world-view is not applicable to our modern way of life. And I shall go on trying as long as I have the strength to do so. After all, if I didn't, I would have to own up not only to the fact that she is right but also to the terrifying situation you and I find ourselves in today. And if we are going to admit the existence of a hell, then we ourselves are paving the road to that hell.

Let's just take, for example, the matter of child-raising. I'm speaking not just for myself, but for all others in the same boat, and I think there are quite a few of us.

I was an average pupil in school; my father punished me every time I got a poor mark. It wasn't just a matter of keeping me from playing outdoors with other kids, or buying some toy — it was more severe than that. And all this struck fear into me — a fear greater than the strap. I was always in fear of something bigger. And every time I stepped up to the chalkboard, it was like stepping up to the scaffold. And I used to tear pages out of my *dnevnik*...[2]

Marvellous schooldays still ringing —
Textbooks and notebooks and singing!
So fast and fleeting, alack!
No one can now bring them back.
Will they then vanish without any trace?
No, none can ever their mem'ry erase.
Marvellous schooldays!

Remember the words to that song[3] they taught us to make us believe how marvellous our schooldays were? Brainwashing, brainwashing! But we also remember — especially us 'average' kids (and we're the majority, after all) — how glad we were to chuck those hated schoolbags aside just as soon as the summer holidays began!

And just how marvellous can schooldays be for a child who has a physiological need to move around, when here he's required to sit a whole forty-five minutes in a prescribed pose, arms neatly folded on his desk, without hardly moving a muscle? Sure, the slow and sluggish types can take it, but what about the child who is agile, temperamental and impulsive by nature? But under the 'one-size-fits-all' approach, it's as though everybody were robots, no individuality — "Sit there, or else...", the child is told.

And the little fellow sits there, trying to endure the forty-five minutes and then, after a ten-minute break, another

---

[2]*dnevnik* — a notebook kept by each Russian schoolchild with a record of his or her marks, ranging on a scale from 1 (fail) to 5 (excellent). Some children would tear out pages showing lower marks so that their parents would not see them.

[3]*that song* — a school song learnt by nearly all Soviet schoolchildren in the second half of the twentieth century. The words were written by Evgeny Dolmatovsky (1915–1994) and the music composed by Dmitry Kabalevsky (1904–1987).

forty-five, then a month, a year, ten years, and the only way out is to give in. Most importantly, to resign himself to the fact that he will have to keep resigning himself to things his whole life long. He will have to live the way society dictates, marry the way society dictates, and go to war directly the order is given. He must unfailingly believe in anything he is told.

People who willingly resign themselves are very easy to control. Only it's best if they're physically healthy and up to all sorts of tasks. But then they start drinking and taking drugs. But doesn't a Man do this to escape, even for a moment? Doesn't he try to escape from his prison of utter subjection to something his heart and soul cannot possibly comprehend? They don't, in fact, pass all that quickly, those schooldays — they drag out in torture periods of forty-five minutes each.

Our great-great-grandfathers, grandfathers and fathers believed — and we today believe — that that's how it should be, that the child is basically ignorant, and that he must be forced into things for his own good. And so today our children, our Vanyas, Kolyas, Sashas and Mashenkas[4] attend school too, and we today, just like our forefathers centuries ago, believe that we are sending them there for their own good, for knowledge and the Truth. This is where we must *stop!* Let's think seriously about it.

Let us remember Russia in the pre-revolutionary days. Our great-grandfathers are sitting at their schooldesks, not yet grown-up children. They are taught religion, history and what kind of life they are supposed to lead. Those that don't learn by rote — or are slow to grasp the proffered world-view the way they're told to — get a sound drubbing on their hands or head from the teacher, 'for their own good'.

---

[4] *Vanya, Kolya, Sasha, Mashenka* — diminutive forms of *Ivan, Nikolai, Alexander/Alexandra* and *Maria* (i.e., typical Russian names) respectively.

But then the revolution comes along, and all of a sudden adults acknowledge that what the schools have been teaching the children is rubbish and brainwashing. Everything old is thrown out of the classroom, and a new indoctrination takes its place: "Religion is sheer nonsense. Man is evolved from monkeys. Put on red scarves,[5] form up in lines, read poetry and, above all, glorify communism." And so the Pioneers glorify communism, read poetry at the top of their lungs and give honour to adults. "For our happy childhood we thank you, our native land." And once more those who don't try hard enough are subjected to deprivations, beatings and public condemnation.

But then, in our own era, before our very eyes, all of a sudden new directives are handed down: "Take off the red scarves. The Red Plague overcame us. Communism — that's nothing but terror and hypocrisy. Man from monkeys? Sheer rubbish. We have a different progenitor now. The Market! Democracy! This is Truth!"

Where the Truth is, and where false dogma — is still by no means clear. But children once again are sitting at their desks without so much as a stir. And over by the chalkboard still stands a teacher as strict as can be...

For ages children have been under the shadow of a 'spiritual sadism'. Like a ferocious beast, invisible and frightening, it tries to chase each newborn child as quickly as possible into a kind of invisible cage. The beast has some faithful soldier-allies — who are they? Who is spiritually scoffing at our children? Scoffing at every Man that comes into this world? What is their name? Their profession? What? — can we simply accept that their name is 'schoolteacher' or 'parent'? An

---

[5] *red scarves* — red silk scarves worn (during the Soviet period) by the so-called 'Pioneers' (schoolchildren 10–15 years old), whose uniforms bore a superficial resemblance to those of the Boy Scouts and Girl Guides in the West.

educated parent, perhaps? There's no way *I* can accept that right off — what about *you?*

Today in Russia teachers are not being paid their wages on time. The teachers are on strike. "We won't teach the children," they say. Tell me, is it good or bad when someone is not paid the wages owed them? Of course, it's bad. After all, people need something to live on. But what if there are actually 'spiritual sadists' among those on strike? Now tell me, is it good or bad not to give money to those who scoff at your child?

Anyway, the teachers' strikes gave me pause for some rather interesting reflection. Right now all the major cities have private schools, whose organisers select the most talented teachers and pay them a decent wage — in the neighbourhood of twice what they would get in regular schools. Not all parents manage to get their children into a private school, even if they have enough to pay for the tuition. Simply because there are not enough private schools to go round. And why aren't there enough?

The answer is simple — because there aren't enough good teachers. The founders of private schools can't find them.

Another question. If they can't find teachers even at a good salary, who are all those people on strike? Now *there's* a question for you. Only please believe me, I'm in no way wishing, out of the whole cross-section of our society, to point the finger at teachers alone. When I speak about them I'm including myself too. After all, I'm one of them. I too, after all — as a parent — made my daughter study what she was taught in school, and then, when *perestroika*[6] came along, I asked her:

---

[6]*perestroika* — the policy of restructuring the economic and political system of the Soviet Union, initiated by Gorbachev in 1985, which eventually led to the collapse of the Soviet system and the break-up of the USSR in the early 1990s.

"What is your teacher telling you about history now?"
to hear in reply: "The teacher talks, but it's, like, he isn't saying anything." And what could I say to my daughter about that? So I simply advised her: "Well, don't go philosophising about it. Just get on with your studies."

Today we have strikes, but is it only the teachers? Doctors are on strike, so are miners, so are academic researchers. The strikers write on their placards: "Down with the government!" "Down with the president!" It's all quite logical, according to the strikers. After all, if there's no pay, it means the authorities are not carrying out their duties.

Everything in their demands seems logical to us today, but what about tomorrow? Again, a question to be answered. Perhaps it will come out tomorrow that the government and the president have been standing on the bright side all along, saving the whole Earth from invaders and vampires. Perhaps against their will, unwittingly, risking loss of power under a hail of malevolence by their refusal to give money to sadists and destroyers of people's souls and bodies, as well as the Earth. And yet the latter have hysterically portrayed themselves as martyrs in the public's eye.

Today it's martyrs. In the context of today's positions and dogma. But tomorrow there will be a different dogma, and who will be portrayed as what is not yet clear. Anastasia says:

"Everybody is choosing an unreliable path for themselves. They always get what is coming to them, not in the next life, but in this one. But with the dawn of each new day each one of us is given the opportunity to determine whether their path is true or not, and the choice is up to you! You are free to choose which path to take. You are a Man! Become consciously aware of what you really are! You are a Man, born to be in paradise."

I asked her:

"Where is it, that paradise? Who's been leading us into some kind of swamp?" And she replied:

"Man creates everything for himself."

Just try to fathom what she said next! She was affirming, after all, that the time has now come for the speeding up of some kind of processes in the Universe. And those whose way of life does not correspond to the natural laws of being will be subjected to trials — at first in the most ordinary way — clear and understandable, and these trials will serve as a good sign for becoming consciously aware of their actions and the path they are following. For those who don't manage to do this, more troubles will ensue, and then they will have to forsake life in order to be regenerated as healthy beings — but only after nine thousand years.

And it turns out, according to her, that miners tearing open the veins of the Earth, modern medical doctors thrusting themselves into genetic engineering, scientists inventing deadly products — all these have already been shown the first sign in the form of their rejection by society and their failure to achieve financial peace of mind. Those of them who possess material goods today suffer even more from lack of moral satisfaction, as they are subconsciously aware of how harmful their activity is and how it is bringing no real good to anyone.

I tried to object, arguing that coal was needed for factories, but she countered:

"What factories? The ones that smoke and burn up the air intended for Man to breathe, and turn out steel to make machine guns and bullets?"

In other words, she maintains that the system we have created to provide artificial conditions for life is so imperfect that all its present achievements will result in terrible cataclysms.

The ground that has been dug up beneath our large cities — where natural underground streams and pure springs welling up from the depths of the Earth have been replaced by systems of pipes and taps — is unable to restore itself and is rotting away, bringing this rot along with the water into everyone's taps. Anastasia went on:

"The time will come when mankind will understand. The most important scientists will come and pay a visit to the grandmother on her plot of land. Famished, they will ask her to give them a tomato for something to eat. The scientists and their illusory creations are not needed by that grandmother today. She knows nothing of them herself, nor does she want to know. She lives a quiet life without the scientists' help, while they cannot live without her. They inhabit a world of fruitless illusions, leading nowhere. She is with the natural earth and the whole Universe. The Universe needs her, it does not need them."

I tried to object that, if we don't produce weapons but only take care of the land, we'll become weak, and risk being easily conquered by technologically advanced powers that do have weapons.

"They are having a problem protecting themselves from their own weapons!" replied Anastasia. "And from the social cataclysms these weapons engender."

"Sure," I said, "they will abandon everything and come after our grandmothers on their plots of land — come after your *dachniks* — with their machine-guns, and our grandmothers will have no machine-guns of their own to fight back."

"But will they get that far? What do you think? Will they not fight to the death among themselves over our grandmothers?"[7]

So there you have it. If we're not going to argue with Anastasia and simply trust what she says, then we have to

---

[7] *fight ... over our grandmothers* — The Russian phrase here involves a play on words; it can also be understood in the sense of *fight over money.*

admit to ourselves that we're complete idiots, nothing but fruit-hungry worms. That's not something we're willing to own up to!

So, not understanding, perhaps, everything in Anastasia, I am trying to find at least some sort of justification of what we have been creating in our world. And should I not be able to find any reasonable justification, should I be obliged to admit that the path we are following is completely untenable, then... And what then? Let's think about it a bit. Perhaps we should give our children the freedom to grow up without our dogma. And then ask the children where and which way *we* should go.

Anastasia talks about how children whom we have not corrupted spiritually will find the way to winning salvation for both themselves and us or, rather, to attain the paradise given us right from the beginning.

It turns out everything in our world is simple, yet not so simple. Why — tell me — why not extend the experience of Academician Shchetinin's school to other places? Why not set up at least one such school in every major city? Well, it's not all that simple, it turns out. I asked Shchetinin to set up such a school in Novosibirsk, and he agreed. But who is going to provide the space? A good question. I asked Shchetinin:

"And what if people can be found in other cities to set up a foundation, would you be able to organise at least one such school in various cities?"

"It's impossible to settle everything right away, Vladimir."

"Why?"

"We shan't be able to find that many teachers for all the schools."

And again the thought: What's this about there not being enough teachers?! Who are all those people out on strike?

Academician Shchetinin's school is a regular government-supported institution, it's not a private school. It comes under the Ministry of Education of the Russian Federation and does not charge tuition fees.[8] But why is it located far away in the mountains, in a ravine? Why? And why was there an attempt on Academician Shchetinin's life? And why was his brother killed? And why do the Cossacks[9] help guard the school? Who doesn't like this school? Who is it interfering with?

I was invited to a meeting with the Education Committee of the State Duma.[10] Officials there had read the first two books — *Anastasia* and *The Ringing Cedars of Russia.* And there were people on the Duma Education Committee who shared and understood Anastasia's views. Good people. I told them about Shchetinin — they know him very well, and have great respect for him.

"Then what's the problem?" I asked. "Why is nothing changing in the educational system in this country? Children are suffering as they did before — every time they step up to the chalkboard it's like going to the scaffold. And they still sit at their desks without stirring."

I was saddened by their response, which, unfortunately, has tragic consequences for those who are still children today. Paradoxically, it is the teachers, the teachers themselves who have turned out to be an insurmountable barrier, as I heard and understood this gruesome reply:

[8]Despite Shchetinin's school's official status, since this book was published in Russian in 1998, the Russian Orthodox Church has labelled the school a "totalitarian sect" and it has become a target of a concerted libel campaign in the mass media (described in Book 7 of the Ringing Cedars Series, *The energy of life*) aimed at discrediting the school and disrupting its operation. In 2001 the school's main building burnt down for unknown reasons but was rebuilt by pupils themselves in an even more impressive form.

[9]*Cossacks* (Russian: *kazaki*) — descendants of a race of independent professional warriors who traditionally hired out their services to the ruling authorities, especially in the Caucasus.

[10]*Duma* (pronounced *DOO-ma*) — Russia's national parliament.

"What would become, tell me, of the whole raft of academic titles and degrees, the countless dissertations on the subject of child-raising? What would become of our research institutes? After all, they've worked out a whole system. The machinery has been set in motion, and its flywheel can't be stopped with the wave of a wand. Anyone who has defended a doctoral thesis, especially one who has achieved professorial rank, is going to stick as hard as he can to his own views."

I also learnt how a woman member of the Duma lamented after visiting Shchetinin's school:

"I don't understand anything that's going on in that school. It's quite out of the ordinary — something like a sect."

I wasn't aware of the specific meaning of the word *sect* (Russian: *sekta*). Later I looked up the definitions in the dictionary, which read as follows:

Sekta (Sect) — from Latin *secta* — teaching, movement, school.

    1. A religious community or group which has cut itself off from the prevailing church.

    2. An isolated group of people absorbed in their own narrow group interests.

It is not clear in what sense the Duma member was using this word, but I feel neither definition is really applicable to Shchetinin's school. And if it has indeed cut itself off, has it cut itself off from the good or the bad? I think, if it has cut itself off at all, then it has detached itself from the sadistic treatment of children. As for the Duma, as long as its members make such statements, I have nothing to say. Let readers themselves consider whether and in what measure the second definition quoted above applies to certain factions in the Duma: "An isolated group of people absorbed in their own narrow group interests". Does that mean they're a sect?

Shchetinin was shot at. But he is a man. Now the Cossacks, perhaps, will help to some degree. And Anastasia promised to protect the 'new shoots'. Now I realise it would be better for her not to come out of her taiga, at least for the time being. If she were just slightly more aggressive, she could easily zap dissertations, academic titles and all sorts of rot with her ray. But no way! "A gentler approach," she says, "is needed. People's consciousness needs changing."

Anyway, here I've gone and written down my thoughts about child-raising and our modern schools, only they've come out rather chaotic, not very sincere. Not very sincere, since if I were to describe how I really feel about our schools I'd have to resort to some pretty foul language. But my style of writing has somehow changed after my talks with Anastasia. There are a lot of words that simply wouldn't fit in.

I would still like to say a word to all those teachers who have been able in spite of the system to impart to their children even a smidgen of good and, as Shchetinin says, "enrol them in the natural cosmic process". *Thank you!* Along with my deepest respect!

And there's another thing I have learnt from what Anastasia says about child-raising — namely, that first and foremost comes the conscious awareness of the child as an individual. By comparison with us adults youngsters are, of course, physically weaker, but at the same time immeasurably kinder than we are, unsullied, not bound by dogma. And before we go filling children's heads with any kind of moralising, we need to understand something about the world ourselves. *Ourselves!* We need to think things through ourselves! And to forget about somebody else's dogma, at least for a time.

As for us entrepreneurs, we too have to somehow seek out teachers in each city, help create foundations for the schools where we shall be teaching our children and grandchildren.

CHAPTER TWENTY

Mediums

Day after day my stay in the taiga goes by, and I can't find any particular activity for myself. Anastasia keeps running off, still tending to her own affairs. Our son, even though he is still quite little, splendidly copes with everything through the help of his 'nannies' of the wilds. It's a strange turn of events: as though humanity has thought up so many activities simply to give it the feeling that it is doing something. And out here all you do is go for walks in the forest and think. So I take walks, and I think. Now I've come once more to the lake and sat myself down in my favourite spot by the shore, underneath a cedar tree. And I'm looking at the bag of readers' letters and thinking I'd better not forget to have Anastasia answer all these questions. As soon as she approaches, I ask her:

"You see these letters from readers? I've sorted them all out according to the type of question. There are questions on child-raising, various suggestions, questions on different religions, on Russia's purpose, on war, there's poetry and greetings, letters from mediums. You see?"

"Yes, I see."

And the first thing I did was to ask Anastasia about mediums.

"There are people who say — in fact, they write in their letters — that they communicate with extraterrestrial civilisations, with certain individuals in the past, that they hear different voices, and some record what they hear — they say that they record various kinds of information communicated to them by the Supreme Mind of the Universe. We have books published in huge print-runs on 'channelling' — contact through mediums.

Above: An autumn view of a clearing in the Western Siberian forest. The tall evergreen tree in the center is a Siberian cedar (*Pinus sibirica*). Photo © 2007 Vladimir Konjushenko.

Below: A view of the Siberian taiga near Novosibirsk. Photo © 2007 Sergey Pristyazhnyuk.

Above: Main entrance to Shchetinin's school (Tekos, Russia). Photo © 2004 Dmitry Samusev.

Right: A pupil decorating the wall of a new administrative office. Photo © 2004 by Vladislav Kirbiatiev.

Left: Pupils at a self-guided learning session. Photo © 2004 by Marina Kolmogorova.

Above: Shchetinin's pupils perform a folk dance in the auditorium they themselves designed, built and decorated. Photo © 2004 by Alexey Kondaurov, Nizhny Novgorod, Russia.

Below: Pupils at Academician Shchetinin's school, 10–15 years old, are building a new hall on their campus in Tekos, Russia, without adult supervision. Photo © 2004 by Vladislav Kirbiatiev, Grishino eco-village, Russia.

Above: Martial arts performance by Tekos pupils. Photo © 2004 by Alexey Kondaurov. The school curriculum includes a wide variety of subjects, ranging from traditional disciplines to folk dancing, self-defence and architecture. Pupils are fully involved in the life of the school, from cooking meals to construction and self-governance.

Below: Pupils' choir performance at one of the school's regular concerts. Mikhail Shchetinin standing in front with accordion. Photo © 2004 by Vladislav Kirbiatiev.

Above: Like everything else on the campus, decorations at the main entrance were designed and executed by the pupils themselves. Photo © 2004 by Alexey Kondaurov.

Left: A typical session: learning without teachers. The school is not divided into age-based forms or grades, and students learn efficiently without adult supervision.
Photo © 2004 by Vladislav Kirbiatiev.

Details of the school's interior design. As with everything else on the premises, the pupils are fully responsible for the design, construction and decoration of all buildings. Photos © 2004 by Dmitry Samusev.

Top: Residents of Novosibirsk planting cedar trees in the spring of 1998. Photo from the Internet, author unknown. *Bottom:* Siberian cedar sprouting in New York City. Photos © 2005 by Ilya Kurkin.

Readers' art inspired by *Anastasia*: *This is not a dream* © 2006 Maria Ignatieva (above) and *Birds* by Andrey and Natalia Patokin (below).

Blavatsky,[1] for example — there's a woman writer by that name who has written quite a few weighty tomes along this line. And then there's the Roerichs,[2] known to a lot of people — they've written books and produced paintings which have been exhibited in many different countries where their books are read. Other people are afraid, terrified when they hear voices. Look — here's a letter from a little girl in the town of Klintsy[3] — she has a voice telling her he's a wise teacher and she should listen to him, and the girl is afraid and is asking for help. Are people like this really communicating with someone and how does it happen?"

"Tell me, Vladimir, what do you consider to be an extraterrestrial civilisation?"

"Well, I would say the population of some other planet or star, or something invisible existing quite close by. If people can communicate with individuals who lived in the past, it must mean these individuals reside in some kind of invisible world."

"Every Man, Vladimir, is so constructed that he has access to the whole Universe — both visible and invisible. Every Man may communicate with anything or anyone he wishes. It works pretty much the same as through your radio receiver.

[1] *Elena (Helena) Petrovna Blavatskaya (Blavatsky)* (1831–1891) — Russian charismatic spiritualist writer who travelled the world in the 1850s and was especially intrigued by the religions of the Orient. In 1873 she emigrated to America, where she wrote her monumental *Isis unveiled* (1877) and along with Henry Steel Olcott (1832–1907) and William Quan Judge (1851–1896) founded the Aryan Theosophical Society of New York. In 1878 she and Olcott went to India and founded a Theosophical Society there; they later did the same in Europe (London and Paris), where Blavatsky's other major work, *The secret doctrine*, was published in 1888.

[2] *Roerichs* — see footnote 5 in Chapter 17: "Put your vision of happiness into practice".

[3] *Klintsy* — a town south-east of Briansk, just north of the Ukrainian border.

There are so many stations broadcasting all kinds of information, out of which the owner of the receiver must select what he is going to listen to.

"Man is both the receiver and its owner. And which source finds a reception in his thought depends on his conscious awareness, his feelings and purity. As a rule, a Man receives directly information he is able to make sense of, understand and use. And all this must take place calmly and quietly, without intrusive attention drawn to greatness.

"When voices draw attention to their own greatness, they try to appeal to one's sense of self-importance: 'Look here, I'm so great, yet I have chosen only you out of everyone — you shall be my pupil, and you too shall be greater than everyone else.' As a rule, this is what you would hear from inferior, soulless creatures. They are not granted a bodily existence, so they attempt to oppress the human soul and occupy another's body. They act on Man's mind, his sense of self-importance and his fear of the unknown."

"'But how do we save ourselves from such creatures?' — many readers are asking."

"It's really very simple — they themselves are cowards, rather primitive cowards at that. You need to give them an ultimatum: 'Get out of here, and if you do not, I shall burn you with my thought!' They know very well that Man's thought is many times stronger than they are.

"Another thing you can do is chew a celandine[4] leaf, but first you should put the leaf in the palm of your hand and say to it mentally: 'Save me, little leaf, from all impurities'."

"But what if a whole lot of people want to talk with the same source? What happens then? See, a lot of people say in their letters that they talk with you — is that true? And if so, how do you manage to answer everyone? After all, there are a lot of them, and they all claim that they talk directly with you and you answer them."

"Every individual produces their own thoughts. And everyone's thoughts still exist — they do not simply disappear into oblivion. What you and I think also exists in space — my dream is there, too, and my thoughts, and everyone who wishes to can hear them — many can hear them at the same time — it is only a question of the degree of distortion the receiver is capable of permitting."

"What do you mean by *distortion*? What determines that?"

"It is determined by the purity of the receiver. Imagine, Vladimir, that you are hearing someone speak over an ordinary receiver. But instead of distinct words you get interference, static, and you do not know what some of the words are, and the concepts behind them are unclear, what do you do then?"

"Well, then I try to guess what words might fit into the gaps where I don't understand."

"Exactly. But a word you put in might change or detract from the original thought being conveyed by the sounds, or could even turn it in the opposite direction. Only one's own purity is capable of hearing Truth undistorted, and if they are insufficient — your tuning and your purity, that is — then you should not blame the source.

"In your material life, in your world, there are a multitude of sources of sound on all sides, all of them claiming to be Truth and trying to control your mind and will, to make your

---

[4]*celandine* (from Greek *khelidon* = swallow) — here referring to *greater celandine* (*Chelidonium majus*), a yellow-flowered plant whose blooming is associated with the arrival of migrating swallows, and whose leaves and flowers are used as medicine. Native to Europe, Eurasia and North Africa, it has also been naturalised in North America. In Russian the greater celandine is known as *chistotel*, derived from the root *chist-* (signifying 'pure' or 'cleansing') and *-tel* (signifying 'body') — a name consistent with its traditional use as a cure for a variety of skin diseases.

___ ___: their own purposes, but you are free to listen to them or not to listen. You are free to decide, with nobody to blame but yourself."

"Let's say that's true," I observed, "but what if there is some kind of question for which there is no answer in all the Universe? Let's say you're asked a question, and you don't have any thoughts out in space on that subject to respond to the question, and you yourself haven't produced any thoughts in response to that question, what then?"

"A question for which there is no answer in the Universe will immediately speed up the evolution of everything. Like a flashbulb bright and clear as a bell, it will reach into all corners of the Universe and everything will be set in motion as well, there will be a rejoining of opposites, an answer will be born and it will be heard."

"So, that means, right off you'll hear the question and glimpse the one who's asking it?"

"Just like everyone else, I too shall hear it right off. But unfortunately, for centuries people have been asking the same questions over and over again — there are answers to them, but not many people who hear those answers."

"But how can I tell what's what? How can I tell when the source is communicating Truth, or rather, when Truth is being perceived without interference? After all, there's no crackling sound in one's ears when we hear something externally, and you say that the answer is born, as it were, in the form of our own thoughts — thoughts we produce ourselves. But what helps us tell whether the voice we hear is a good voice or no? After all, everyone that hears voices thinks they are listening only to the Supreme Mind."

"It is when you hear more than just words. When suddenly there is a flash of feeling or emotion in the soul and tears of joy in your eyes. And when sensations of warmth and fragrances and sounds are born in you. When you feel within yourself the impulse or urge to co-create and a thirst for purification, you may be sure that you are clearly hearing the thoughts of Light.

"When it is simply cold information that comes, an order or command, even one that talks about good — perhaps it seems wise, even very wise, and the originating source claims to be supreme and very powerful — know this: it is not good that is hiding behind good, but an entity not accorded a place in perfection that is trying to persuade you to follow it for its own purposes."

CHAPTER TWENTY-ONE

Should we all go live in the forest?

"Anastasia, here's another issue. Some readers want to live the way you do in the taiga. Several are trying to come to see you and are asking directions, others want to organise settlements in the taiga. And they are sending in their proposals to the Moscow Research Centre as to how to do this. Besides, I've read that there are already settlements like this elsewhere in the world, where people leave their homes in the city and settle in communities in Nature. This is happening in India, in America, and also here in Russia — in the Krasnoyarsk[1] region, for example. And people are asking you the best way to realise their dreams."

"But why go to another place to live?"

"What do you mean, why? People are leaving the dirty cities where the air quality is poor, where there's a lot of noise and bustle. They are moving to places that are clean and ecologically pure, so they can become purer themselves."

"But back there where it has become dirty, who is to clean it up? Others?"

"I don't know who. But is it so bad when Man has the desire come to him to live in a clean place in Nature?"

"The desire is a good one, that is not the point. When a person who creates dirt around himself comes to a clean place,

---

[1]*Krasnoyarsk* — a major industrial city of approximately one million inhabitants in central Siberia, a few hundred kilometres east of Novosibirsk. Krasnoyarsk is also a port on the Yenisei River which, like the Ob in Novosibirsk, flows north to the Arctic Ocean.

he pollutes that place with his very presence. You need to clean up the place you've been polluting first, thereby washing away your sins."

"So, everything starts with a clean-up, eh? And how do you suppose that's all going to happen?"

"Conscious awareness is the point of departure for any venture. The aspiration of one's thought finds the most effective path, just like any stream in Nature.

"It is all happening already in Russia today. Look closely, Vladimir. You will see that the factories with their smoking chimneys are not doing very well — that is not by chance, it did not simply happen that way all by itself.

"Another thing — there is less and less money for the nation's armed forces.

"But the main thing is that you have stopped treating as heroes people whom it would not be a sin to call vandals — people who have polluted the Earth by their actions.

"There is no need to go live in the forest. The space of the forest will not be quick to accept newcomers, and will take a long time examining their motives, habits and way of life. After all, the place where you were living, the place where you are living now — all that was once a forest too, planted by the Creator. And what has become of this beneficial oasis of paradise today?

"People who go live in the forest are no more significant — indeed, they are less significant — than the dachniks who plant gardens on desolate, abandoned land with their own hands. They are known and loved by every blade of grass on their plot, which endeavours to give back to them the warmth of the Universe. And the true feelings are to be found in those who themselves have set up this oasis of paradise, giving embodiment to the good in their souls amidst the bustle and gloom of death."

"But what then will become of the cities?" I queried. "Who will maintain those in a state of normalcy? After all,

everything in the cities will decompose into a void, everything will decay and be destroyed."

"There should not be a sudden transition from one base
to another — a gradual movement is needed, and it is already
taking place. It is splendid, and it will be even more splendid
in the future."

"Well, Anastasia, you are true to form! Just like before, all
the dachniks are still your idols. The only thing is, they hardly
ever talk about spiritual things, the way a lot of different religious organisations and communities do."

"Are words needed when their deeds are holy?" Anastasia
countered.

"Here are some more letters," I offered. "One person has
already sent me five letters. He claims that he hears voices
and that his dowsing-rod tells him you are summoning him to
the taiga, and he is trying to get to you; he threatens me and
goes to see Solntsev at the Moscow Research Centre.[2] He
says we are concealing you from everyone and demands that
we organise a trip for him to come see you in the taiga. And
he's not the only one. How would *you* answer him? I think
you know these people are in love with you. They think they
should be with you, doing good deeds together. And live together with you in the taiga."

"I would respond to everyone who is sincere: thank you for
your love. But I have not invited anyone to the taiga. What
would you do here? What could you contribute? If your intentions are good, let them be expressed right there where
you are living. Let your love illuminate those living around
you."

---

[2]*Alexander Solntsev, Moscow Research Centre* — see Book 2, Chapter 25: "The
Space of Love".

CHAPTER TWENTY-TWO

The Anastasia Centres

"In cities in Russia and even abroad," I told Anastasia, "people have already started organising centres named after you. Let me read you just one example of the many letters my daughter Polina has been receiving. She herself has answered a number of them, and sent others to me, but I can't possibly reply to them all, and there are some letters I'm not completely sure how to respond to. After all, there are people out there who think these centres represent some kind of sect. Just listen to this letter from one of the centres — how would you respond?"

I took one of the letters Polina had forwarded to me and read it to Anastasia in full. Here it is:

Hello, Polina!

I am a member of our school's Anastasia Ecological Creativity Centre, Valery Anatolievich Karasiov.[1]

Our Centre is still quite young, it was set up on 4 December 1997 and is now in the process of getting established. Its genesis was facilitated by your father's book, for which we are all very grateful to him.

Anastasia, like a ray of Light in a dark realm, is now bringing together the creative forces of us adults and children who have not lost our creative capacities, with the aim of standing up for our honour and dignity. Such people as we aspire to bright ideals and believe that the happiness of Russia, our native land, is in our hands and our thoughts.

---

[1] *Karasiov* — pron. *ka-ras-YOFF.*

We realise how right now the forces of darkness are pressing down upon her, and we are trying to help her as much as we are able.

Teachers, schoolchildren and their parents are all working togeth-er at our Centre.

At the present time we are introducing Anastasia and her ideas to kids and their parents with the help of classes and seminars, making use of your father's books and distributing them along with magazine articles.

We are also trying to put together a collection of scientific accounts explaining Anastasia's abilities.

We are aware of the challenges involved in the task of awaken-ing Man's conscious awareness, in overcoming the inertia of human thinking, and so we are going about our activities with calmness and confidence. And we have already made some interesting discoveries.

Some people we have been in touch with look upon Anastasia as a beautiful fairy-tale, while others tune in to our work right from their very first reading of the book. There are also a few who are starting to spread rumours that Anastasia is just another sect, which makes us smile.

But as it has been said, "Father, forgive them; for they know not what they do."[2]

The main thing is, we are so happy that Anastasia has brought us together in this rural region with its dying agricultural industries and its decaying state-run farm, whose managers have completely forgotten about people's needs — especially young people's needs. And this has all happened on the very spot where Mikhail Kalinin[3] *was*

---

[2]Luke 23: 34 (*Authorised King James Version*).

[3]*Mikhail Ivanovich Kalinin* (1875–1946) — as Chairman of the Soviet National Executive Committee in 1922, the USSR's first titular Head of State. In 1931 one of Russia's oldest cities, Tver (founded in 1135), and subse-quently the Tver region (*oblast*) — where this letter is coming from — were both re-named *Kalinin*, and retained this name throughout the Soviet pe-riod. The city's historic name was restored in 1990. One of the ships in Vladimir Megré's river fleet was also named the *Mikhail Kalinin* (see Book 1, Chapter 1: "The ringing cedar").

born and the hugely successful *Verkhnyaya Troitsa*[4] *state-run farm once flourished.*

Here at the Anastasia Centre located at the M. I. Kalinin rural school, our Raduga[5] programme was initiated. It is designed to work out and put into practice creative solutions for the development of our native land, work education and the moral upbringing of the rising generation, to set up a basis for the manufacturing of ecologically clean agricultural products.

Raduga also aims to set up a young people's cultural and ecological manufacturing co-operative under the name Rus, which will include the Slavic cultural centre known as Lada and an ecological manufacturing complex called Rod.[6]

This is the kind of programme Anastasia helped us set up.

Let unbelievers believe in their unbelief, but we shall work on bringing our programme to fruition, no matter how unrealisable it may appear to some people.

Our goal is to allow our young people to feel the practical results of their creative forces.

One aspect of the Raduga programme involves getting to know our own country better — studying our native land's ancient history and the life and culture of our Slavic forebears.

---

[4] *Verkhnyaya Troitsa* — the name literally means 'Upper Trinity', although to the Soviet authorities in charge of the farm the term was strictly geographical. Workers on state-run farms (*sovkhozy*) received a monthly wage, just like factory workers. This was in sharp contrast to the period preceding the collectivisation of the 1930s, when peasant households owned their land and whole families often participated in the farm labour.

[5] *Raduga* — the word literally signifies *rainbow*.

[6] *Rus* (pronounced *ROOS*, rhyming with *moose*) — the name of the Old Russian territory, which by the 9th century A.D. was centred around Kiev; *Lada* — the name given to the Slavic goddess of love and beauty, also related to the word *lad*, signifying *peace, union, harmony*; *Rod* — an ancient Slavic name for God as Creator of all (see footnote 10 below).

A long time ago, right near Verkhnyaya Troitsa, the town of Medved was built, but hardly anything is known about it — it has literally been wiped off the face of the Earth. Along the banks of the Medveditsa[7] River may be found old Slavic burial mounds. We are wondering whether some of these have a similar significance to that of the dolmens[8] in Gelendzhik, since that was where the local Medved militia did battle with the Tatars and their Golden Horde.[9] We need this information, as we don't want to be neglectful of our past. We shall take steps to preserve whatever we can, and do at least a partial restoration. That is our request, Polina, to Anastasia.

In the spring we shall start setting up a nursery to cultivate cedar seedlings — this will be possible thanks to one of our local residents, a forest warden by the name of Georgi Shaposhnikov, who gave us this amazing gift.

Our children's theatre, headed by Tatiana Yakovlevna Zaonegina, who comes from Siberia, will be putting on a play based on the Anastasia book. The kids are really fired up with the project.

We would very much like other centres and organisations Anastasia helped come into being to get in touch with us. May her Divine lines of Light join all our centres together throughout Russia.

Mutual communication, even if just through letters, will increase our strength and enable us to find answers more quickly.

Our postal address is as follows:
Anastasia Ecological Creativity Centre
M.I. Kalinin School

---

[7] *Medved, Medveditsa* (pronounced something like *mid-VEYTCH, mid-VEY-dit-sa*) — these names both signify *bear* (the animal), male and female, respectively.

[8] *dolmens* — See Chapter 4: "Score for the Universe".

[9] *Tatars* (= Tartars), *Golden Horde* — a reference to the Mongol invasion of Russia under Batu Khan (grandson of Genghis Khan) in the 13th century; the Tatar domination of Russia lasted almost two hundred years.

Verkhnyaya Troitsa, Kalinin District,
Tver Oblast 171622

*The following is a gift from our school to all for whom Anastasia
exists.*

HEAR YOUR ORDERS,
DEAR BROTHERS!

To help with Anastasia's
World-happifying ideas,
To head off disaster for good
And never repeat it, we should
Awaken at six in the morning,
So as not to find anything boring,
And with smiles and sincere open hearts
We shall stretch out our arms to the stars
And draw ourselves close to her side —
To our mother dear, as to our bride:
"Here I am, your own blood to embrace!"
And a sly smile creeps over our face...
In an instant, not a moment beyond,
We see Mother's own face respond.
"To you, Mother Nature, good morn!
Who with God the Father[10] *have borne*
Strong warriors — where would one find
In the Universe any more kind?

---

[10] *God the Father* — The Russian term is *Rod-Batiushka. Batiushka* is a tender
name for 'Father', while *Rod* is the name ascribed to God by the ancient
Slavs to designate the source of all life. Many current Russian words are derived from this root, including the word for *Nature* — *Priroda,* whose literal
meaning is 'attached to God'.

Oh Sister, of Slavic blood true,
So long we have waited for you.
We all have been touched by your Ray:
Your orders we now will obey."
Dear brothers, your orders now hear!
At six, like the book says, dark fear
Will flee from our forthright attack —
Fifteen minutes it takes, there and back![11]
So that no threat will vex our dear sister,
We must give this child our assistance.
We answer to them, after all.
Then how can we not heed their call?
We are quite used to lending our aid
To break through the dark foe's blockade![12]

Valery, a Russian naval officer

I wish you success and all the best, Polina. We at the Centre shall be happy to receive any information you can give us about Anastasia. Please give our very best wishes to your father.

Happy New Year!

[11] *fifteen minutes* — This whole poem is a reference to Anastasia's 'orders' (an urgent request, at least) to "wake up in the morning at a set time — six o'clock, say — and think about something good. ... They can think about their children, about their loved ones, about how to make everyone happy. If they could only think fifteen minutes like that." See Book 2, Chapter 8: "The answer". The word *orders* harks back to the observation by the 'colonel' in Book 2 (Chapter 20: "The Ringing Cedars of Russia") that Vladimir was "not good at following orders properly".

[12] *blockade* — a reference to the 900-day Nazi blockade of Leningrad (starting in September 1941), which was broken by the will of the Russian people — first, during the winter months with the 'Road of life' across frozen Lake Ladoga east of the city, and then for good, finally ending in January 1944. During all this time the city never surrendered and was never taken by the enemy.

"Well, Anastasia, what do you have to say about this letter?"

"I can say that it shows marvellous aspirations of the human soul. But neither you nor I can take credit for that. It is beauty and the strength of their soul that alone are responsible. Their names would make an even worthier choice for naming the centre. I grew up in the cradle of the Creator, while *their* soul has strived to brave the tortures of hell and has survived.

"For years a string of hardships, deprivations, temptations and commotions have tried as hard as they could to distort their realisation of good. Their souls have been able to overcome it all. They are stronger than those who have cut themselves off from the world behind a stone wall. They are in the world and have enriched the world with their presence. *They* should be remembered in the centre's name. If people plan to name all the centres after me, it will result in the formation of a cult, and that must not be. A personality or image cult always distracts Man from the essential thing, from himself."

"Then what will be the result?" I queried. "There's Solntsev's centre in Moscow and Larionova's in Gelendzhik, and already I've heard people speak of an Anastasia division at the International Academy of Spiritual Development. How will people be able to find out with precision what these centres are all about?"

"Intuition is a quality given the same to all, Vladimir, and a centre's real essence and attraction is determined not by the name: it is the soul that should be able to feel one's actions."

"Now that's an interesting turn of things, now I'll have to do some more thinking. You are a quite unconventional woman, Anastasia, and conversing with you makes thinking work not just for me but for many others around too, and when is there time to relax? There is one more concrete question they ask of you: what kind of burial mounds are located there on the river, on the Medveditsa?"

"There is no need to excavate the mounds. They have fulfilled their task, and people were born there who were the first to ask the most important question."

"What question?"

"Think about it yourself, Vladimir, please. But I shall tell you this for now: you go show people like these the ways to make better contact with each other. You can do your part by noting their addresses in your book. Let all the letters, like bright rays, help them warm each other's hearts. The St Petersburg poet Korotynsky[13] gave you a hint a long time ago when he wrote:

> *This ray of Love from heart to heart*
> *With thread Divine will gleam and glisten,*
> *Make every soul from dust depart*
> *And thirsting minds with heaven freshen."*

"Okay, I've got it," I said. "I myself was going to publish both the letters and the poems readers have sent in. I wanted to keep them and release them in a volume of their own. I myself felt there was something deeper than usual in them. And I can make their addresses known through the Moscow centre, so that people may end up helping each other. My daughter Polina can also participate — she has been very good about taking care of the letters to date.

"You know, Anastasia, it might not be a bad idea if people from all over the world could carry on communication with each other. They will find people of like spirit and like mind,

---

[13] *Alexander Korotynsky* — a St Petersburg scientist and poet. See Book 2, Chapter 25: "The Space of Love".

they can marry or at least become friends, they can start new common trends or spend their vacation together. Right, that's it! That's great! I'll get a selection of letters together and put them out as a collection.[14] You know how our newspapers now offer a dating service — people place advertisements, let's say they're looking to meet a potential marriage partner, and they give their height, their age and the colour of their eyes, as though they were selecting a prize cow for breeding. But here, I wager, it will be much better, when people meet in spirit and start helping each other."

"Of course a union in spirit is better, more solid indeed."

"Yes... But there's just one problem..."

"A problem? What is it?"

---

[14]A 544-page volume of readers' poetry, art and letters was subsequently published in Russian, under the title: *V luche Anastasii zvuchit dusha Rossii. Narodnaya kniga* (The soul of Russia sings in Anastasia's ray. A people's book). It was followed by half a dozen issues of a periodical known as *Almanakh "Zvenjashchie Kedry Rossii"* (The Ringing Cedars of Russia Almanac). Most letters and poems are now shared through numerous on-line forums and e-mail lists, as well as on the pages of periodicals specially devoted to readers of the Ringing Cedars Series.

CHAPTER TWENTY-THREE

Re-creating Shambala

"For some reason it all happens like that in Novosibirsk — it just happens that most people who are critical of me and my book come from there. Indeed, that's the only place people criticise me.

"My first book is already being published in three foreign countries, and in many others contracts are being drawn up. But in Novosibirsk all they do is curse it. My daughter Polina is there — I can only imagine what she's going through. And as for a collection of readers' letters, they'll only say: 'What new thing are you dangling in front of us now? Why don't you go back to your own business?'

"They did a programme recently on Novosibirsk TV about the early entrepreneurs.[1] I was included, and in the course of an interview with my daughter they asked her about my absence from my business. Polina tried to explain something about my spiritual interests, but they cut her off."

"Just a little more time will go by," Anastasia replied, "and most residents of Novosibirsk will think highly of both you and the book. The best of the friends you had last year will come back, and new friends will appear.

"In one of the city centres a short way from the Eternal Flame[2] your friends both old and new will plant a brand new avenue and name it *Cedar Allée*."

[1] *the early entrepreneurs* — i.e., following *perestroika* and the collapse of the Soviet system in late twentieth-century Russia.

[2] *Eternal Flame* — in memory of the soldiers from Novosibirsk who fell during World War II.

"Sure they will! Come on, now! You'd better think again —
a 'Cedar Allée' near the Eternal Flame? You're really quite the
schemer, Anastasia, dearest little dreamer of mine!"

She jumped up from the grass and stood on her knees,
beaming all over, throwing up her hands, and all of a sudden
whispering:

"Thank you for those words so fine — 'dearest', 'mine'.
That *is* me you were talking about here, Vladimir, right? Have
I indeed become dear to you?"

"It's more just a figure of speech we use. But still, your
dream is very beautiful."

"And it will come about, believe me, it will. Just as I dreamt
it, that is how it will turn out."

"But nothing comes about in the world all by itself. Now
if you could attempt to create some kind of miracle in
Novosibirsk... No, not just any old miracle — what's the
point of a miracle which leaves people neither hot nor cold?
If only you could grant, say, that every resident of the city became just a little bit richer and healthier — in other words,
so that everyone in Novosibirsk could be happier — now for
that, perhaps, people might plant an allée. But I have an idea
that all your forces of Light, even all told, would still not be
able to bring that about, Anastasia. That is not within the
grasp of anyone's might."

"You are right, Vladimir, nobody has power over Man's
will. Man must still work out his own plan, his own destiny,
whether it be for joy or sorrow. Each one's conscious awareness will point out the path to follow."

"But who then is toying with our awareness? Who is im-
peding us from choosing the path leading out of sorrow to
joy?"

"Why grope for causes outside your own self, Vladimir? In
accusing others, what do you hope to change? A feeling so
great has arisen within you: to create something good for the

citizens of your city — I find it very appealing. It is a thought I myself now must dream with...

"Ah! Great indeed! I have it! Yes, that is it! All the people of Novosibirsk will go down in the history of our nation, for it is there that a generation of happy people will be born. Every one living there today will become happier right away.

"Let us think together what we can say to the people of this whole city you are concerned about, how we can learn to break through to each one's heart and soul..."

"And what do you want to say to each one of them?"

"That together they will all be able to re-create Shambala."[3]

"And just what might this Shambala be? Elaborate more precisely."

"People have been looking for æons for a holy place on the Earth. They think that it is called Shambala, that anyone there can link with the wisdom of the Universe. But no one has ever been able to find Shambala, though seekers have galloped through many foreign nations looking for it. And find it they will not, as long as they look for it therein, for ever since time began, Shambala has been re-created — both within each one and in its outward manifestation — by Man."

"More specifically," I interjected, "what must be done to establish a link with the wise Universe and to make one happier — show me a step we can take here that lies not within ourselves? All that's within ourselves is somehow unclear. Show me some outward things we need to sow, build or break?"

"Let each resident of the big city obtain a little nut from a resinous cedar cone, place it in his mouth and hold it there in his saliva. Let him plant it in a little pot of earth in his home

---

[3] *Shambala* — a Tibetan word indicating 'the source of happiness'. See footnote 1 in Book 2, Chapter 27: "The anomaly".

and water the earth every day. Before watering he should put his fingers in the water, and should be in a good humour. And the main thing — he should be wishing good for himself, his children and descendants, and a conscious awareness of God. This he should do every day.

"When the seed sprouts, one may share with it one's innermost thoughts. On summer days and frost-free nights the little pot with the little sprout should be placed outdoors among other plants growing in the ground so that it can commune with stars, the Sun and the Moon, so that it may know the rain and the breeze and the spirit of the blades of grass all 'round, and then come back again to its friends, its parents. This may transpire many times now, while the desire is there and time allows.

"The seedling will grow and develop through the ages — a cedar, after all, will live more than five hundred years, beget offspring and tell the young cedars about the soul of those that cultivated them. When the sprout has grown in the home to about thirty centimetres, it may be planted in the earth in early spring. Have the city authorities allot at least one square metre of earth for their sprout to all those that have no plot of their own.

"And these sprouts will be planted around the edge of the city, among the houses and in the centre of busy squares. Let each person take care of his sprout and help each other in this.

"From the ends of the Earth people will come to this city to see and touch the sacred trees, and exchange at least a word or two with these happy people."

"Why would people suddenly start coming here from all over the world?" I asked. "Now if only you could discover some kind of new sacred sites in Novosibirsk! Dolmens, for example, as in Gelendzhik. You told about the dolmens of Gelendzhik, and now seekers from various Russian cities and other lands are flocking to see them. I noticed that every day now they have tours to the dolmens.

"And every year in September readers from many places come together for a conference. Artists organise exhibits, and they record things on video. And now, surprise of surprises, trees are growing in the city. Well, not actual trees yet, just cedar seedlings."

"These will not be ordinary seedlings," Anastasia pointed out. "They are like the *ringing* cedars. Warmed by the kindness of human hearts, having touched the human soul, they will take in the best rays the Universe has to offer and start giving them back to Man. And Man and the Earth together will begin to shine once more in that place — now and forever. And there will come a new conscious awareness, and discoveries of universal importance will go forth from such people through the whole Earth!

"Do you know what a sacred site is? Believe me, Vladimir, you will come to know one in your own native city."

"That's all very tempting, of course," I said. "But you know, Anastasia, there's hardly anyone that's going to take your word alone. There's no way this can be known from our history books, and it's not something our modern science is going to condone. Now, if there were just something a little more influential than you, someone better known with the proper credentials, who could show this..."

"The Koran makes some wise statements on the significance of trees. Buddha too got this wisdom when he went off for a long time into the woods. Tell me, Vladimir, you have been reading the Bible, have you not?"

"Yes I have, what of it?"

"The Old Testament notes that long before Christ Jesus' birth the wisest of the Earth's rulers, King Solomon, used cedar wood to build a temple to the glory of God and a house for himself. He hired a work force of considerable size to cut down the cedars and bring them in from far-off places. King Solomon was very wise, as the Bible says, and the Song of Songs he wrote has come down to us as an oasis of wisdom in the present day.

"The Old Testament also tells us that toward the end of his days the wives of his harem from various lands and various faiths began leading Solomon away from his faith. He came to know a variety of faiths. And do you know which one satisfied him the most?"

"Which one?"

"The one where trees are not only cut down but also planted. And on his death-bed this wise king comprehended that his temporal house and temple would be destroyed, that his descendants would not be able to maintain their power or greatness. It would mean that the might of his kingdom would lapse into a void. And it all came about exactly as he had foreseen.

"And to this day his soul is dismayed by the great mistake he had made. And the wise king realised that it was impossible to do a deed pleasing to God, and at the same time take the life of any of His own creations. The torment that affected his soul and many human souls extends through whole millennia, as they watch one mistake making itself again and again over thousands of years. But the mistake can be corrected, and then a splendid dawn will once more rise over the world. News of your city will spread through all the channels of the Earth and the Universe.

"Of all the miracles on Earth that have come down to us today, nobody has ever heard of a city where every citizen thereof cultivated trees such as these this way — with extraordinary love and tenderness of soul, thereby transforming their own city of stones into a true, living temple of the Universe, into a Space of Love. For this a whole conscious awareness is needed of the Divine, so may it, oh may it rise up so fine and good within each one's heart, and do its destined part to help the Universe be understood."

"Perhaps, just perhaps, there is a germ of rationality in what you've said, Anastasia, and I shall, perhaps, write about it, so that people may determine everything for themselves, but I must warn you that you're missing something here. You spend all your time carrying on about trees... But... well, how can I put this? You'll never be able to get married officially. You don't have the documents you need to take your turn at the Civil Registry Office, and here you're talking with such earnestness about trees. As it is, the church clerics consider you a heathen, and when I write these words of yours, they won't even let you in the nearest church, and certainly will not officially wed you to anyone."

"Vladimir, *do* write down my words, let people read them and decide for themselves. And do not be ashamed of these words, humble your pride. Not everyone, perhaps, will understand the meaning of these words, and not right away. But in your city there are many scholars who will supplement in scientific words what I have begun to say, if you believe that people will understand them better than my own words. And then there are the journalists. Do not be angry over their criticism; not all the journalists have had their turn. And if the time should ever come for me to wed, believe me, Vladimir, one will be found to hold the crown above my head."

"And what if people create something like that in another city, other than Novosibirsk?"

"Any city can be reborn. For achievements like these to be fulfilled, a different conscious awareness in people must be instilled, and when it appears, the face of cities will be changed for years to come. But among them there will be a first to perceive the Grace."

"Blessed Anastasia, you are so naïve, it seems, you never have anything but bright dreams. Well, okay then, I shall write what you say, so that people will know these things too."

"Thank you, thank you! I do not know how else to thank you."

"What for? That's not hard to write. You can add something more, if you like."

"I ask you, people, do not just read what I say as empty words, you need to make sense of what you have heard."

"Here you are, Anastasia, answering questions from readers, and you speak of Man as a creator, but you're a woman, don't you see? You know what the leader of one of our religious denominations said about women?"

"What did he say?"

"He said that women are incapable of creating — their proclivity, then, is to look beautiful and inspire men to various achievements and creativity, but it is only men that do the actual creating."

"But you, Vladimir, do you agree with statements such as those?"

"One could agree with them, I suppose. You know about statistics, which is an impartial science. Well, if you go by statistics, you come up with this—"

"What?"

"Andrei Rublev, Surikov, Vasnetsov,[4] Rembrandt and other famous artists were all men — there simply aren't any women among them — at least, I don't recall any women artists. The

---

[4]*Andrei Rublev* (pron. *roob-LYOFF*) (1365?–1430?) — one of the best-known early Russian painters, known especially for his icons and frescoes. His images are considered to convey a sense of humanity and deep spirituality. *Vasily Ivanovich Surikov* (1848–1916), a member of the *Itinerant* (*Peredvizhniki*) school of Russian art, known for his huge paintings of historical Russian battles. *Viktor Mikhailovich Vasnetsov* (1848–1926) — another Itinerant, who also painted monumental historical canvases (his younger brother Apollinari was not only a fellow artist but an archæologist as well).

inventors of the airplane, the car, the electric engine, the space satellite, the rocket-ship — they're all men, too. Right now one of the most popular art-forms in our society is the cinema, and in order to produce a film you need a director, and he's one of the most important figures in film-making. And once again, all the best film directors are men. Occasionally you find a woman director, but they're very rare. And unlike men, they don't produce any really outstanding films. And the best musicians are invariably men, just like the philosophers — both the ones we know from antiquity and in our modern world — they're men, too."

"But why are you telling me all this, Vladimir?"

"Well, I just had a thought. Maybe it'll help you."

"What is your thought? Could you share it with me?"

"It's like this. Maybe you, Anastasia, should concentrate more on some kind of home improvement here, along with child-raising, and not burden yourself down so much with concerns about the outside world and other people — after all, *men* can take care of everything there. Men alone, according to statistics, which is an exact and impartial science. Historically, too, all the important things have been done by men, and we can't get away from history. Do you understand how irrefutable this argument is?"

"I understand what you are saying, Vladimir."

"Just don't you go and get upset, now. Better understand everything right off the bat, so that you can busy yourself with your own affairs and not with those that others can do better. You're trying to change the world for the better, but only men can do *that,* you see — they are better inventors and better creators than women. Do you agree?"

"Vladimir, I agree that men appear outwardly to be creators. If you look at it from a material viewpoint, that is."

"What do you mean, 'outwardly'? And from what other viewpoint can you look at irrefutable facts? You'd better not get philosophising here. Just tell me out-and-out: can you at least create *something*? For example, can you at least do embroidery? Can you embroider a beautiful design on a piece of fabric with a needle?"

"I would not be able to embroider a design with a needle."

"Why not?"

"I would not be able to take a needle in my hands. A needle that has been manufactured out of the depths of living Nature. What is the point of creating something if it involves first destroying a great, living creation? Think, Vladimir, when a demented person takes a work by one of the Great Masters, as you said, and rends the canvas to pieces to cut out rabbit figures, would you call his actions *creativity*, making an allowance for his dementia? But if another person, this one rational and aware of what is around him, did the same thing, then his actions would be defined in quite a different way."

"How?"

"Think about it. For example, his actions could be termed vandalism."

"Come on, now, you're not serious?! Does that mean that all creators and artists are vandals?"

"They are artists and creators in their perception of the world as seen on their own level. But if their consciousness should rise to a higher level, they would create by entirely different means."

"And what 'different' means would these be?"

"The means by which the Creator has created all in His own impulse of inspiration. And the power to perfect His creations and to make new creations of their own is something He has given to Man, to Man alone."

"And just how did the Creator create everything? And what instrument did he give to Man for creativity?"

"Thought is the chief instrument of the Great Creator. And thought has been given to Man. Creations are true when thought is brought to fruition through the soul and intuition and feelings, and the main factor here is and will always be: the purity of one's awareness.

"Look how the little flowers thrive at our feet — their splendid shapes and colours and tints are constantly changing in creation alive. These are something you can perfect with your thought. Concentrate, try to change them, give them a better look."

"What look? For example?"

"Indulge your fantasy, Vladimir."

"Well, I can at least do that. Let this camomile here, for example, take on one red petal, and the next one stay as it is, so the alternation will make it better, more cheery."

And all at once Anastasia fell stock still. She began concentrating her gaze on the white camomile. And you know, the camomile — slowly and quietly as could be, but still, right before my eyes — began to change its colours. There they were, alternating — first there was a red petal, then a white, then a red one again. At first the red petals were barely noticeable, then the colour became stronger, and the red hue kept getting brighter and brighter until finally they were simply blazing with a shining red radiance.

"You see how it happened, Vladimir — you came up with the idea, and I created it all with my thought."

"What are you saying, Anastasia — that everybody can do this?"

"Yes! And they are doing it. But they use material for this, which they first slay, and dead material can only deteriorate. So mankind through the ages has struggled to stop his creations from deterioration, even as human thought becomes more and more preoccupied with just plain rot, and Man has no time to think about what constitutes genuine creation.

"Every thing is preceded first by thought. It is only with time that it gets embodied in matter or the changing strands of the social order. But whether they are creating for better or for worse — they do not immediately understand.

"Look how you wanted to change the colour of the camomile's petals. I changed them with my thought — the camomile obeyed Man's thought. But look closely now, did you really think up something better? More perfect than it already was?"

"In my view, it's splashier and more cheerful."

"But why are you not excited when you talk about the new Creation?"

"I don't know, maybe it's because there's still something lacking, maybe some kind of colours — I can't tell right now."

"The colours have come into conflict with each other — the tenderest tints have paled for the sake of splashiness. A loud splashiness fails to evoke calm and tender feelings."

"Okay, okay. Try to change everything back the way it was."

"It is not *I* that shall do it, but the camomile itself will be able to. The red will fall away. After all, we did not slay the camomile. It is alive. Nature itself will bring everything back to a state of harmony where it can thrive."

"So, in your view, Anastasia, are all men ignorant vandals and are women the creators?"

"All men and women are one — in each of them two principles merge into a single one. And in the creativity they feel, they are inseparable — earthly existence is there for them both."

"But how can that be? I don't understand. I, for example, am only a male of the species."

"And what do you consist of, Vladimir? The flesh of a male and the flesh of a female have merged into one, they are united in you; similarly the spirit of two has merged into one spirit within you."

"Then why do people go and state in treatises exactly what a woman is and what a man is, and state which of them is stronger and more important?"

"Think about it yourself, who would want to, and for what purpose, replace your awareness — your consciousness which the Creator gave to everyone in the beginning — with his own dogma?"

"Well maybe the Creator just happened to give someone more than others, and this person, as a teacher, is striving to share his wisdom and awareness with everyone?"

"Every little sprout on the Earth — the seed of a birch tree, a cedar tree or a flower — is filled with the knowledge of the Creator. So how could the thought come to you that the Creator could deign to withhold something from His Supreme Creation? What could be more insulting for a Father than a complaint like that?"

"What are you talking about? I'm not complaining about anyone. I was just consulting with myself, thinking out loud."

CHAPTER TWENTY-FOUR

Who are you, Anastasia?

Before asking Anastasia this question, I took a good look at her. Here sitting before me was a woman — a young and beautiful woman, hardly different in her outward appearance from many others in our modern civilisation. Perhaps it is just that her body conveys a lightness — barely perceptible, even outwardly — in the way she stands, the way she moves her hands, and especially when she rises to her feet and walks, all of which she does with an extraordinary lightness.

The burdened, ponderous gait of a 'senior citizen' is noticeably different from the movements of a young, energetic, vivacious person. But that gives you some idea of the difference between the way Anastasia moves and walks and the motions of even the trimmest of our young athletes. She gives the appearance of being light as a feather on her feet, yet physically very strong. She easily carried my heavy backpack fifteen kilometres, at the same time helping me make my way along.

During our brief stops she didn't lie down, or even sit down in exhaustion, but kept moving — either running off to collect herbs, or massaging my wounded leg. And she did all this with a sense of lightness, cheerfulness and a smile. Where did this vivaciousness come from all the while?

Just try observing some time the flood of people walking along the street — take a look at their faces. I did. Almost all of them look absorbed in thought, downcast or just plain glum. Especially when a person is walking all by himself along a road. Even when they aren't carrying any heavy load, and they're neatly dressed, evidently not starving, since they're smoking expensive cigarettes, and yet their faces are marked with tension, weighty thoughts — and there are many like that, the majority in fact.

Anastasia, on the other hand, never allows her smile to leave her face. She constantly delights in the Sun and the grass, the rain and the clouds, like a carefree child constantly beaming with gladness, and even when you talk about serious matters with her, she betrays no sadness.

Just like now... But *no,* her appearance at the moment was not typical at all. Anastasia was sitting there, her head slightly bowed and her eyelids lowered, like someone upset or even a mite depressed, as though she could sense what I was about to ask. But I still asked her:

"If you look at all the letters, Anastasia, you will get an idea of all the different things people call you — even an alien from another planet. In one of her books the well-known psychologist and writer Oksana Lavrova[1] has called you a biologist from an extraterrestrial civilisation. Ordinary readers call you a goddess, but strangely enough, those who call you that also write as if they were talking to a close friend. You are probably the first person to be addressed both as a goddess and a close friend (without genuflection) at the same time.

"Most scholars and religious leaders call you an *essence,* an elevated essence, or a self-sufficient substance.

"Look, here I've been talking with you all this time, I've written a book about our conversations, and I still can't figure

---

[1]*Oksana Vladimirovna Lavrova* — founder of a psychological consultation centre named *Squaring the circle* (*Kvadratura kruga*) aimed at making a range of psychological services more familiar to the general population. She also heads a professional training institute known as the Samara College of Practising Psychologists, located in the city of Samara (a major port on the Volga River south-east of Moscow).

out just who you are. Can you yourself give an explanation to me of who you are — clearly and precisely?"

"Vladimir, whom do you see in me yourself?" Anastasia asked, without raising her eyes. "And why is it so important to you what other people say?"

"The thing is, that I myself don't even know what I'm looking at. To be honest with you..."

"Say what you have to say honestly and sincerely, Vladimir, and I shall try to comprehend it all."

"Well, okay, I'll say it out-and-out... The first time I saw you, Anastasia, you gave the appearance of being a simple woman. Then that first time I walked with you into the forest, we sat down to rest and you took off your dress and your kerchief and I saw how beautiful and attractive you were — well, you know, the kind of girl we say is sexy or has sex appeal. I really wanted to... well, do it with you — you know what I mean. D'you remember?"

"I do."

"But now, maybe on account of all these complexities compiled thereon, I don't really want it any more, even when I see you with nothing on."

"You've come to fear me, Vladimir, is that it?"

"Not fear you, no, not really. But things have got, well, complicated. You've borne a son, see, but you've become somehow more and more distant, even when you're right here beside me, like you're sitting right now, and still you don't seem very close — you seem far away to me. At least that's my impression. My head keeps telling me you're some kind of 'essence'."

"I may be an essence, but you are an essence, too."

"No. I'm no essence, nobody ever calls me that in their letters. Even if some readers curse me, still, nobody doubts that I'm Man, a human being."

"Excuse me, Vladimir — you know, I am a woman. Which means I too am Man."

"You say you're Man too, but you don't seem to want to do the most basic thing to prove it. You don't want to live the way people live. The way the whole world lives. Everybody wants to have an apartment, furniture, a car, but oh no, not you. There's money coming in now from the book, and soon there'll be lots more. Let's buy ourselves an apartment, furniture, a car, let's go round together and visit the sacred places. We'll take our son along, too. Our society is now restoring the temples and monasteries, and other countries have lots of sacred sites and historical monuments we can visit. But you have nothing here — no sacred sites. What's holding you back? What have you got to lose?"

"Vladimir — this is my Space here. The Creator's creation in its pristine state. My foremothers, my dear mother, along with my forefathers, tenderly cared for every blade of grass with their love, and every majestic cedar remembers their gaze and the warmth of their hands. And in the spring it comes about that the seeds of all the plants bring forth sprouts. And each grain that touches the ground in the spring contains all the information of the Universe. As well as information about how they will see the Light of Grace.

"And the seed grows apace until it becomes a sprout, and the Sun attempts to help it out, and the sprout reaches out to Man for more than just the Sun — it reaches out to Man for the Light of Grace.

"Thus the Creator created all. He designed everything so that Man could continue creating along with Him. My parents saved and preserved the creations thereof, and there is a Space of Love! My parents gave it to me.

"What in the world could be more sacred than the creations of the Creator, of my parents, of living Love filling all Space?

"This is how every Man that is a parent should act. They should give the child born to them the Space of Love!

Marvellous as a mother's womb, only in the Space of Love is there room for their future offspring — indeed the future of their own — to be truly happy.

"It is this holy place and the Space of Love that is my gift to our son."

"You are giving this of yourself, Anastasia, but where is my Space of Love? What can *I* give our son?"

"The links of the continuum have been violated in many people's lives. But the strand is not broken. The strand that ties humanity as a whole and every creature in particular to the Creator needs only to be comprehended and felt by each, and then to each may be extended both light and might. Vladimir, expand the Space of Love. Right there in the world where you now live, create a Space of Love. For the sake of our son, for all the children of the Earth, make the whole Earth into a Space of Love."

"I don't understand. What do you want from me? To change the whole Earth?

"That is exactly what I want!"

"And for all people to love each other, for there to be no more wars or crime and for the air to be pure and sublime? And the water too?"

"Let it be thus throughout the Earth!"

"And only then will it be construed that I am a father true, that I have given something to my son?"

"Only then will you be a father true, worthy of your son's respect."

"Does that mean that otherwise he will not respect me?"

"What can he respect you for, Vladimir? For which of your achievements do you wish to receive respect from your son?"

"For the same reason that children all over the world respect their fathers. Their fathers gave them life."

"What kind of life? When a child comes into the world, where, in what place does he find any gladness? And why, in the space given to him by his forefathers, is there so much sadness? And the child born again must live in this same sadness, and yet the one who gave him life does not surmise that he himself is to blame. And so we live and crave respect, and are surprised when we do not get it.

"Believe me, Vladimir, very few children respect their fathers as they should. This is why, as soon as they grow a bit, they leave their parents by and by, and refuse to remember them, thereby accusing them, albeit intuitively, and repeating in their turn the parents' mistakes. If you wish to earn the respect of your son, Vladimir, you will have to make the world a happier place for him."

"Aha, so... Now it's clear!" I jumped up. My head was ever so filled with despair and anger. My thoughts became jumbled together.

I realised it now, as I hope it has become plain to all: Anastasia is a fanatical recluse. I surmised this right from our very first encounter. Maybe a recluse with extraordinary, unexplainable abilities and perhaps she has an excuse — perhaps these same abilities — her Ray, for example — do not allow an accounting of her own — I mean, do not allow her to take account of her possibilities. You will remember she said she would transport all people across the dark forces' window of time.[2] Well, she herself realised that she was not in a position to do that, and now she is resorting to luring me and my readers into her fruitless vision. I knew for sure that along with being abnormal and fanatic she is incredibly deceptive and makes use of her guile to do whatever she can for her dream!

She bore a child, and she's managed to get a book written by now. And then — something really wild! — she says if I'm to earn the respect of my son, I shall have to make the whole world into a Space of Love to give not only to my son but to

[2]See Book 1, Chapter 27: "Across the dark forces' window of time".

every child!... Methodically and by intricate art she is draw-
ing everyone into her dream and keeps complicating my part
before my very eyes. First write a book, says this girl, then
make a Space of Love throughout the world, and then what?
We have known of more than a few fanatics who have tried
to change the world, and now they are where? Vanished like
smoke into thin air. And here I find another one sitting in
front of me with head bowed, with the same aim in mind: to
change the world.

I knew that it was useless to argue with eccentrics and fanatics, that I needed to calm down and walk away, but I was
unable to prevent myself. And to this girl sitting there on the
ground with downcast eyes, as before, I still said:

"I know now, I realise precisely who you are. You are a mixture of *essence* and *Man*. And you know how to deceive. You
deceive so nicely, you took me right in. Oh wow! what an intricate web of guile you weave! To get me first to write a book
and then entice me by bearing a child.

"You tried with your non-human logic to hide your fanati-
cism, only a hole appeared in your plans. A loophole appeared,
you understand. While I was writing the book, I had the
chance to talk with many people. I learnt a lot indeed, and was
given all sorts of religious books to read. And there's no way I
can tell what *you* know of them, but this one thing I can say:

"Several thousand years ago the world saw wise men of
greatness and piety arise, whose spiritual currents in all their
variety continue to flow until this day. There are more than
two thousand different religious confessions on the Earth,
you see — I learnt this from a recent talk session on TV. They
one and all proclaim the good, they aim to give advice to everyone on how they should live, and every leader tries to make
it known that the path to Truth lies through him alone. We
have our fill of sacred sites all around, but still, has anything
really profound, far-reaching or sincere resulted from their

gabfests over the many, many years? Or from the multitude of their teachings?

"There's just one thing I've understood: millennia pass, but war has never ceased for good. The war of dogma against dogma. The strongest wins a fight and thinks that he is right, but not for long. Time passes, a new war ensues, and a new song, a new dogma gains ascension with its views. But no one thanks the losers in this contention, nobody pays them any attention. I'm saying all this openly and frankly... Do you know who *you* are? Do you know what you are calling me and all the readers to?"

Anastasia arose, looked me calmly in the eye and said:

"You need not go on, Vladimir. Believe me, I know what you still might say to me anon. Let me declare it myself. I can say it more briefly and without swearing."

"Yourself? Well, why not give it a try? And all right, then, without swearing. What was *I* going to say?"

"You were going to say, Vladimir, that there are a multitude of prophets on the Earth, and a multitude of teachers too. There are so many different dogmas it is hard for you to decipher them all. But when I speak, you will be able to understand everything — if you really want to, that is.

"*Water* will prove to be the criterion, the measure of all things. Every day that passes, water seethes with more and more contamination. And the air becomes more difficult to breathe.

"The parade of worldly rulers, no matter what grand temples they might have built, will be remembered only by the filth they have bequeathed to their descendants. The legacy they give makes life more dangerous every day, but we continue to live. You have surmised, Vladimir, that I am one of those who tries to teach everyone how they should live. One of those who creates just another religious denomination, only too ready to put himself at its head.

"But I can assure you now that the sense of self-importance which has ended up burning all that were initially enlightened, is not something I shall ever resort to myself. I shall be able to win and I am winning! I shall stop the factories spewing their stinking dirt, the miners will comprehend that they cannot rend apart the precious veins of the Earth.

"I beg of you, people, change your professions just as soon as you can — all those professions which bring hurt to the Earth, to the great works of the Creator.

"I beg of you, Man, to grasp this fact just as quick as you can, that no one on Earth can be truly happy as long as he keeps causing harm to the Earth.

"Yet a little while and human misery will start feeling the pain of agony, it will burn in its own flame.

"People's conscious awareness will transport them across the dark forces' window of time. Look around, Vladimir, and you will find that what I sought in my dream is already coming to pass, my dream has been caught up by the Universe itself, it is resounding in the hearts of all people, and is already transporting mankind over the abyss, and only the doubters will run amiss and fall into its snare. But mankind, believe me, Vladimir, mankind shall be spared.

"People will see what children can be — people will learn life in paradise.

"The events now taking place in Russia are not coincidental. Assume a closer vantage-point, Vladimir, to observe these events. I am nullifying the portent of doom hanging over the Earth."

"But who *are* you? Who do you consider yourself to be?"

"Oh, do you still not comprehend me in the least? Dogma has instilled in you a distrust of your own soul. Do you still perceive me to be a sorceress, do you still believe my dreams and aspirations to be fruitless? You are inflamed by doubts — you believe in yourself, and yet you do not believe, it turns out. For that I am to blame, unskilled as I am — my speech is too bewildering and confused. But I say to each one of you who reads this: forgive me — I cannot find the words to make myself clear to all without exception. Forgive me, Vladimir, for my deception — not everyone is grasping what you wrote, and some are simply trying to get your goat.

"But how am I to expiate my guilt? I have got it! If you wish, I shall play the fanatic for you to the hilt. Or I can simply show you what I am. You can take it any way you like, but please do believe my one desire: that I sincerely aspire only to good for all.

"I beg you, please do not frown. Smile and see how great is everything around. Do not torment yourself, let nothing anywhere be kept hid. And if it is easier to accept me as a sorceress naïve, feel free to consider me as whatever you perceive."

"Now that's better," I observed. "Things are clearing up again. Does all this mean you've just been playing a game?"

"And have you begun to perceive my play with your Soul?"

"Well, all play ought to involve some fun!"

"Of course you're right in that. I should keep everything light and simple, and fun for everyone."

The Sun's rays shone through the dark clouds on the lake and the shore. They lighted upon the blades of grass and the raindrop-laden leaves, while the raindrops formed intertwining circles on the surface of the lake. Anastasia, who before this had been speaking quietly yet emotionally, her eyes constantly fixed on me, suddenly looked about her, clapped her hands and broke out laughing.

Her laughter was loud, alluring and infectious as it rang through the cedar branches and across the shore and surface of the lake. She began spinning about with childlike excitement, delighting in the rare drops of rain with a girlish, boisterous laughter. But every three minutes or so she interrupted her fiery dance.

I watched as the Sun's rays played in the glistening rain-drops, or perhaps it was in the tears streaming down her face ablaze with colour. Everything around fell still, and Anastasia's sonorous, confident, yet despairing words filled all space as they were carried off into the air. And the air over the taiga took on a greater tinge of blue, and the birds fell silent, too. As though they were listening to all her words as off into space these flew.

"Woe unto you, prophets! For centuries you have been proph-esying about the frailty and futility of earthly existence, terrify-ing people with doom and hell's flaming judgement. Tame your ardour — you are the ones that have made Man's comprehen-sion of Heaven so much harder!

"Woe unto you, Nostradamus! The dates of the fearful cat-aclysms upon the Earth were not so much your divinations as the creations of your thought. You made millions of people persuade themselves of these by what you taught and thereby aim their thoughts at the implementation of the same. Your thought still hovers up there, hiding in the blue, still frighten-ing people with your prophecies of despair, but now they will no longer come true. Let your thought join in fray with mine. Of course you knew all this ahead of time, and that is why you are so eager to flee away.

"Woe unto you who call yourselves teachers of human souls! You try to suggest to Man that he is abject and weak in spirit, knows nothing of himself and that all Truths are acces-sible only to a few elect like yourselves — and only through worshipping *you* can he detect God's voice and the Truth of the creation of the Universe. Cool the passions of your heart, and may everyone now know: the Creator has given all to each one right from the start, and we need only refrain from hid-ing the Creator's great creations under the murky domain of dogma and conventions, the murk of inventions for the sake of one's own selfish pride. Stand not between the people and

God. The Father wishes to speak with each one equally. The Father abides no intermediaries.

"The Truth has been there right from the start in each one's soul. Not tomorrow, but here today each Man may be happy and whole! The Creator has filled each moment of every year with gladness. And in His thought there is no room for His beloved child to feel torment from sadness."

Just listen to her play! So inspiring! Yet so despairing! Of course she's playing, but why above her in the sky over the taiga is there shining bright such an extraordinary light? As though the heavens could record every inspiring and despairing word that from this forest recluse upon the Earth could be heard:

"Woe unto you, prognosticators of the ages, foretelling but gloom for Man, thereby creating both gloom and hell! Oh, how earnestly you have been feeding your own *egregor*,³ frightening people in the name of the Father and more. Well, here I am. You can all come to me. With my Ray I shall take but a moment to burn up the murk of age-old dogma. All anger on Earth, leave your deeds and make haste to me, join fray with me, try your utmost.

"But you, militants of all faiths, it is you who have created all the wars. Dream about wars no longer. Lure not people into war with your obscure deceptions for the sake of your own mercantile connections. I stand alone before you. Try to defeat me. To defeat me, all of you come meet me together. The fight will be fightless, as clergy of all religious confessions will greet me with their merged assistance.

³*egregor* (also spelt *egregore*) — a non-material collective psychic entity or field uniting members of a human group or organisation (e.g., religion, state, association), generated and maintained by thought energy of the members of the group. Egregor can, in turn, influence the psyche of the members of the group and, taking on life of its own, persist even when the original members leave the group.

"Foremothers of mine, Fathers of mine, imbue them with the True Light. Give them everything you have been so carefully saving for *me*. Give freely to all who are able to accept the Light.

"Let evil join fray with itself and with my flesh, not with my soul. I give the whole of my soul to people. In people I shall prevail through my soul. Prepare yourself, all wickedness and evil-mindedness, to leave the Earth behind and fall upon me!

"I am Man! I am a *Man of pris-tine or-i-gins*. Anastasia I am. And I am stronger than you."

"Stop!" I shouted, thinking that it was some kind of game, continuing all the while to play itself out. "Why are you taking it upon yourself to call up all these vile things?"

"Vladimir, be not afraid of them, they are cowards every bit. Besides, you yourself said that I was deceptive. Deceptive? Yes, deceptive indeed. I have outwitted them. They were mocking you, treating me as an invention of your imagination, while all along I was involved in creation. And the strength which my foremothers and my fathers showed, which they had brought with them from their pristine origins, I have now bestowed on many people."

Anastasia stamped her foot and chortled out loud, and then spun round again, just like a ballerina. And I got carried away with her play and began giving her my moral support.

"So go to, Anastasia, burn them! Let all the evils of the Earth throw themselves at you and you will burn them! Only be careful, don't get burnt yourself!"

"To dispose of me, Vladimir, they would have to let go of many of their earthly gains, free many human souls from their chains.

"But even if I should perish, my dream shall come to pass all the same. The strings of the harp of the Universe have struck up a happy strain, and human souls are hearing them. They understand them!

"Sound forth, O Universe! Sound forth with your happy strain! For them, for all the people of the Earth. May everyone know the melody of the Soul!

"Look, Vladimir, human Souls are sending their rays to the weary Earth."

With these words Anastasia ran over to the plastic bag with the readers' letters, dropped to her knees and placed her hands on the package. And with childlike joy and enthusiasm she exclaimed:

"When an elderly man, a soldier who had been in the war, read your book and tears suddenly appeared... When a young mother's whole attitude to her newborn child changed overnight... When a young girl, about twelve years old, saw everything clearly for the first time and started to love life... And look, when a young man stated he would no longer take drugs and went home to his mother...

"When people send you letters from prison, you can see and feel how their souls sing, and they take on a whole new strength...

"These are all signs I found that people's souls are understanding the combinations of the sounds of the Universe, now they are resounding in their thoughts, and they are accepting them... Not all of them yet, but there will indeed be many! And the heavens know thereof and wait to meet each one with love.

"Look, just look how people are expressing their understanding in their poetry."

She was so sincere in her delight and kept talking about the letters, that I got carried away with the scene before me and thought: Well now, let her have her joy, let her play her little scheme and believe that her dream will come to pass. I shall tell everybody about her playing. She thinks up everything herself and delights in every thought.

I was trying to calm myself down, when suddenly in my consciousness everything again got jumbled together. I began once more to dismiss everything as her own caprice and fancy, yet there was one thing, can you imagine, that simply blew my mind away. Can you imagine, she talked about things that really were in those letters! And even in the letters I hadn't brought with me to show her! But how could she know? After all, she hadn't read them.

I watched and listened in absolute astonishment as she read poems that were still in the envelopes, as she took a sudden delight in something or stood preoccupied in silence, as though she had read all the letters together in a single moment.

She kept on talking about the letters with complete accuracy. Complete accuracy... Stop! So even before this, then, she must have been describing everything else with complete accuracy, too. It hadn't been a game at all... Was she dreaming? Of course she was dreaming! But she had also dreamt before — about the book, and people's poetry, and now all this lay right there before her eyes. Wow! Her dreams really did come true! They actually came true!

The book was lying right there in front of her. A material object.

Fantastic, indeed!

No, this can't be real!

Dear reader, are not you too holding in your hands right now a part of this despairing recluse's dream, materialised in a book?

And what next?

Can it be that everything else may actually come to pass?

When I got over my initial sensation of amazement, I asked her:

"Anastasia, how did you know what people had written in their letters? It was as though you had read them all. And even those I hadn't brought with me!"

Anastasia turned around, all beaming with joy:

"It's all very simple, on the whole, how one can hear what is being said by the soul."

And all of a sudden Anastasia fell silent. And in this silence she walked calmly over to me and said thoughtfully:

"It is not that hard to answer all the questions, but the answer still will not take away the problem, as one question but begets another. Right now mankind keeps biting into Adam's apple, not realising that this will never fully satisfy him. Besides, anyone may hear the answer for himself within."

"And how may each one recognise when the true answer comes, as opposed to one that is not so true?"

"Only one's sense of self-importance can lead people about, lead them away from the Truth. Vladimir, try to hear me out."

We sat down on the grass beside the package containing the letters. I saw how her eyes were sparkling, and there was a rosy blush in her cheeks, as she said:

"I shall tell you about *co-creation*, Vladimir, and then everyone will be able to provide an answer to his own questions. Please listen carefully, Vladimir, and write about the Creator's great co-creation. Listen and try to take it in with your soul..."

And thus began Anastasia's inspired account of co-creation. But it is a long one. And no room to include it here right away. But this one thing I'll say: after I heard it I really did want to pray.

With my sincere respects to you, dear readers, and until we meet in the next book,

Vladimir Megré

To be continued...

Lada's message
In place of an Editor's Afterword

As I was finishing writing my lengthy afterword, my four-year-old daughter Lada, named after the goddess of Love, walked in from the garden, hiding a 'present' behind her back — two cucumbers she had just picked, one for me and one for her Mama. I hardly paid any attention to her approach, immersed as I was in my work. Lada quietly sat on a chair and patiently waited for me to become aware of her presence. She considered it totally unacceptable to interfere with an adult's thought process.

At that moment I was busy compiling citations from the unheeded sages of many millennia ago as well as of the recent past, who have all been trying to convey the same message: simple life in close contact with Nature is an absolute condition of happiness and peace.[1] I had noted how significant it was that the understanding of humanity's deep spiritual connectedness to Nature and especially trees — the understanding that once served as foundation of entire cults and

---

[1] Leo Tolstoy, for example, wrote in his *What I believe* in 1884: "One of the first and universally acknowledged preconditions for happiness is living in close contact with nature, i.e., living under the open sky, in the light of the sun, in the fresh air; interacting with the Earth, plants and animals. Being deprived of these experiences has always been seen as a huge misfortune. It is felt most acutely by people locked up in prison. Just look at the life of those who adhere to the dogmas of today's world: the greater success they enjoy in terms of what the world teaches, the more they are deprived of this precondition for happiness."

cultures[2] — still survives today in folk customs and such universal symbols of rebirth as the Christmas *tree*. I had also been writing about our former much closer relationship with wild animals and gave examples of people living in our world today — such as Tom Brown, Jr.[3] — who, just like Anastasia, can relate to wild animals in the same way we relate to household pets...

I had had things to say on education, too. Just think about it: a century and a half ago — at a time when compulsory schooling had not yet become a "natural" part of our lives — Leo Tolstoy (who, as a proponent of 'anarchical' ideals of love, compassion and non-violence, would later be denied a Nobel Prize in literature) already discerned the havoc wreaked on children by the educational system or by what Megré calls 'spiritual sadism' and founded a school based on freedom rather than compulsion.[4]   And today John Taylor Gatto, a teacher with thirty years' experience and a recipient of numerous teaching honours — including the New York City and the New York State "Teacher of the Year" awards — speaking from his decades of teaching experience and his own extensive investigation of contemporary American education — shockingly declares point blank that the school system has been *deliberately* designed

---

[2]In fact, the words *cult* (a system of religious worship or ritual) and *culture* both derive from the Latin verb signifying *to take care of the land* or *to till*, and reflect the understanding of the sacredness of humanity's connection to the Earth. To the present day the primary meaning of *culture* found in dictionaries is "cultivation of the soil".

[3]See *The tracker* (Englewood Cliffs, New Jersey: Prentice-Hall, 1978), *The search* (Englewood Cliffs, New Jersey: Prentice-Hall, 1980) and other books by Tom Brown.

[4]In Tolstoy's view, "education does not educate, it only spoils", and "the best educational system is having no system at all".   For further details, please see his article "Education and Instruction".

to "dumb children down" and kill their creative potential, so as to turn them into compliant members of a "faceless workforce".[5] Interestingly enough, Gatto also describes the early childhood years, in terms very similar to Anastasia's, as "a prison of games" in which children are confined and children's toys as "suffocating your little boy or girl's consciousness at exactly the moment when big questions about the world beckon..."[6]

Lada apparently thought that as long as she continued sitting quietly, I would never pay any attention to her. And so she gently whispered:

"What are you doing?"

"Writing good words about the new Anastasia book," I said, finally turning my head and looking at her.

"Read them to me."

Responding to her request, I read two paragraphs out loud, and then, remembering Vladimir Megré's suggestion to "ask the children where and which way we should go",[7] I enquired: "Well, what do you think?"

"Papa, it's so long and boring!" came a frank reply.

"All right!" I laughed, sensing I would probably have to make my afterword much shorter. "D'you suppose you could put it all more briefly?"

"You should live close to the plants," Lada said in a very serious tone. "In cities cars pollute air and turds from your toilet flow into rivers and make fish unhappy over the dirty water. And papas have to go away and work for money to buy food to

[5]See John Taylor Gatto's *Dumbing us down* (Philadelphia: New Society Publishers, 1992), *The underground history of American education* (New York: Oxford Village Press, 2001) and other books.

[6]John Taylor Gatto. *The underground history of American education*, p. 383.

[7]Chapter 19: "What to agree with, what to believe?".

eat. Do not cut down trees. God co-created everything. All are His little children.

"You want to go see how huge my tomato grew? And the water-melon's so handsome!" she finished off.

"I do," I smiled and, taking me by hand, Lada led me out into the light of the garden.

Brixey, Missouri, USA
Perun's Day (2 August 2005)   Leonid Sharashkin

THE RINGING CEDARS SERIES AT A GLANCE

Anastasia (ISBN 978-0-9801812-0-3), Book 1 of the Ringing Cedars Series, tells the story of entrepreneur Vladimir Megré's trade trip to the Siberian taiga in 1995, where he witnessed incredible spiritual phenomena connected with sacred 'ringing cedar' trees. He spent three days with a woman named Anastasia who shared with him her unique outlook on subjects as diverse as gardening, child-rearing, healing, Nature, sexuality, religion and more. This wilderness experience transformed Vladimir so deeply that he abandoned his commercial plans and, penniless, went to Moscow to fulfil Anastasia's request and write a book about the spiritual insights she so generously shared with him. True to her promise this life-changing book, once written, has become an international bestseller and has touched hearts of millions of people world-wide.

The Ringing Cedars of Russia (ISBN 978-0-9801812-1-0), Book 2 of the Series, in addition to providing a fascinating behind-the-scenes look at the story of how *Anastasia* came to be published, offers a deeper exploration of the universal concepts so dramatically revealed in Book 1. It takes the reader on an adventure through the vast expanses of space, time and spirit — from the Paradise-like glade in the Siberian taiga to the rough urban depths of Russia's capital city, from the ancient mysteries of our forebears to a vision of humanity's radiant future.

The Space of Love (ISBN 978-0-9801812-2-7), Book 3 of the Series, describes the author's second visit to Anastasia. Rich with new revelations on natural child-rearing and alternative education, on the spiritual significance of breast-feeding and the meaning of ancient megaliths, it shows how each person's thoughts can influence the destiny of the entire Earth and describes practical ways of putting Anastasia's vision of happiness into practice. Megré shares his new outlook on education and children's real creative potential after a visit to a school where pupils build their own campus and cover the ten-year Russian school programme in just two years. Complete with an account of an armed intrusion into Anastasia's habitat, the book highlights the limitless power of Love and non-violence.

Co-creation *(ISBN 978-0-9801812-3-4)*, Book 4 and centrepiece of the Series, paints a dramatic living image of the creation of the Universe and humanity's place in this creation, making this primordial mystery relevant to our everyday living today. Deeply metaphysical yet at the same time down-to-Earth practical, this poetic heart-felt volume helps us uncover answers to the most significant questions about the essence and meaning of the Universe and the nature and purpose of our existence. It also shows how and why the knowledge of these answers, innate in every human being, has become obscured and forgotten, and points the way toward reclaiming this wisdom and — in partnership with Nature — manifesting the energy of Love through our lives.

Who Are We? *(ISBN 978-0-9801812-4-1)*, Book 5 of the Series, describes the author's search for real-life 'proofs' of Anastasia's vision presented in the previous volumes. Finding these proofs and taking stock of ongoing global environmental destruction, Vladimir Megré describes further practical steps for putting Anastasia's vision into practice. Full of beautiful realistic images of a new way of living in co-operation with the Earth and each other, this book also highlights the role of children in making us aware of the precariousness of the present situation and in leading the global transition toward a happy, violence-free society.

The Book of Kin *(ISBN 978-0-9801812-5-8)*, Book 6 of the Series, describes another visit by the author to Anastasia's glade in the Siberian taiga and his conversations with his growing son, which cause him to take a new look at education, science, history, family and Nature. Through parables and revelatory dialogues and stories Anastasia then leads Vladimir Megré and the reader on a shocking re-discovery of the pages of humanity's history that have been distorted or kept secret for thousands of years. This knowledge sheds light on the causes of war, oppression and violence in the modern world and guides us in preserving the wisdom of our ancestors and passing it over to future generations.

The Energy of Life *(ISBN 978-0-9801812-6-5)*, Book 7 of the Series, re-asserts the power of human thought and the influence of our thinking on our lives and the destiny of the entire planet and the Universe. It also brings forth a practical understanding of ways to consciously control and build up the power of our creative thought. The book sheds still further light on the forgotten pages of humanity's history, on religion, on the roots of inter-racial and inter-religious conflict, on ideal nutrition, and shows how a new way of thinking and a lifestyle in true harmony with Nature can lead to happiness and solve the personal and societal problems of crime, corruption, misery, conflict, war and violence.

The New Civilisation (ISBN 978-0-9801812-7-2), Book 8, Part 1 of the Series, describes yet another visit by Vladimir Megré to Anastasia and their son, and offers new insights into practical co-operation with Nature, showing in ever greater detail how Anastasia's lifestyle applies to our lives. Describing how the visions presented in previous volumes have already taken beautiful form in real life and produced massive changes in Russia and beyond, the author discerns the birth of a new civilisation. The book also paints a vivid image of America's radiant future, in which the conflict between the powerful and the helpless, the rich and the poor, the city and the country, can be transcended and thereby lead to transformations in both the individual and society.

Rites of Love (ISBN 978-0-9801812-8-9), Book 8, Part 2, contrasts today's mainstream attitudes to sex, family, childbirth and education with our forebears' lifestyle, which reflected their deep spiritual understanding of the significance of conception, pregnancy, homebirth and upbringing of the young in an atmosphere of love. In powerful poetic prose Megré describes their ancient way of life, grounded in love and non-violence, and shows the practicability of this same approach today. Through the life-story of one family, he portrays the radiant world of the ancient Russian Vedic civilisation, the drama of its destruction and its re-birth millennia later — in our present time.

Vladimir Megré
The Ringing Cedars Series

Translated from the Russian by **John Woodsworth**
Edited by **Dr Leonid Sharashkin**

- Book 1 **Anastasia**
  ISBN: 978-0-9801812-0-3

- Book 2 **The Ringing Cedars of Russia**
  ISBN: 978-0-9801812-1-0

- Book 3 **The Space of Love**
  ISBN: 978-0-9801812-2-7

- Book 4 **Co-creation**
  ISBN: 978-0-9801812-3-4

- Book 5 **Who Are We?**
  ISBN: 978-0-9801812-4-1

- Book 6 **The Book of Kin**
  ISBN: 978-0-9801812-5-8

- Book 7 **The Energy of Life**
  ISBN: 978-0-9801812-6-5

- Book 8, Part 1 **The New Civilisation**
  ISBN: 978-0-9801812-7-2

- Book 8, Part 2 **Rites of Love**
  ISBN: 978-0-9801812-8-9

Published by **Ringing Cedars Press**
www.ringingcedars.com